Technical Writing

Bassim Hamadeh, CEO and Publisher
Bob Farrell, Senior Field Acquisitions Editor
Gem Rabanera, Project Editor
Christian Berk, Associate Production Editor
Miguel Macias, Senior Graphic Designer
Trey Soto, Licensing Coordinator
Don Kesner, Interior Designer
Natalie Piccotti, Senior Marketing Manager
Kassie Graves, Vice President of Editorial
Jamie Giganti, Director of Academic Publishing

Printed in the United States of America.

ISBN: 978-1-5165-1029-0 (pbk) / 978-1-5165-1030-6 (br)

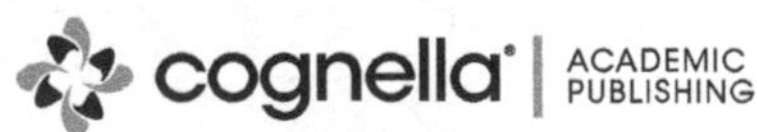

Technical Writing

First Edition

Suzanne Disheroon
Cedar Valley College

Kenneth Price
Texas A&M University—Kingsville

Contents

CHAPTER ONE

Introduction to Professional Writing

WHAT IS PROFESSIONAL WRITING?

As with any type of writing, the most important attribute of a good technical document is that it meets the needs of the reader. Readers of technical documents will have needs that diverge widely from academic readers, whose purpose for reading will be informational rather than vocational, and such readers will be more likely to read every word rather than skim for only the information they need to continue with their work. Academic readers seek deep knowledge of a topic and may read multiple articles that approach a topic from varying perspectives. As a result, readers of academic papers expect essays to include the following:

- In-depth examination of a topic
- Contextualized discussion of a topic that takes into account what others have already said/proven about the topic
- Focused, analytical argument supported by substantial evidence
- Research- or evidence-based conclusions
- Fair and unbiased approach to a topic, with a focus on objectivity, not subjectivity
- Originality
- Accurate adherence to a style sheet, especially as pertains to documenting sources

Readers of technical documents, on the other hand, will typically read with a completely different purpose. Rather than seeking comprehensive knowledge of a topic, especially in today's highly competitive commercial environments, they often seek information that will assist them in completing their task and moving on to the next one.

Further, while academic readers may engage with the texts they select for the purpose of building their knowledge base, readers of technical documents are often looking for specific pieces of information. As a result readers of technical documents value different attributes in what they read. They will appreciate documents that:

- Are brief
- Are clear
- Are concise
- Use straightforward language with minimal jargon
- Include visual cues and hierarchies that identify critical information

While academic writing will most often take the form of essays, technical documents take a variety of forms, including:

- Correspondence
- Proposals
- Instructions/Help/How-to manuals
- Tutorials
- Feasibility studies
- White papers/Knowledge-based articles

Accordingly successful technical documents, regardless of the form they take, will provide readers with sufficient information to accomplish their goals. The documents should help readers spend a minimal amount of time locating the necessary information.

Developing reader-friendly technical documents requires the writer to make a variety of decisions prior to beginning to write, including:

- Topic
- Audience
- Format
- Organization
- Style
- Design

This chapter will provide an overview into each of these areas of technical document development.

TOPIC

In professional settings selecting a topic is typically need-driven. In other words, a technical writer will not sit down to her computer and think, "what should I write about today?" Instead technical documents arise out of a need that a reader has identified or one that the professional writer anticipates before the reader needs it. As a result selecting a topic for a technical document will often take place in the context of a larger project.

For example, if you are part of a proposal team, then a request for proposal (RFP) will determine what topics you need to cover, and the readers of that proposal will have clear and predetermined expectations for the content of that proposal. Correspondence such as an email, on the other hand, will typically be in response to a query from a stakeholder or the need to communicate information to a team. What each of these situations share is the need to provide readers with all of the necessary information so that they can complete their assigned tasks.

AUDIENCE

Meeting the needs of the reader is the single most important attribute of any technical document. A document that does not provide what the reader needs will not be useful, resulting in a frustrated reader and a writer who ultimately wastes his time. Learning everything about your reader before you begin a project will save everyone time and irritation.

Answer the following questions about your reader at the beginning of a project:

- What is the reader's purpose for reading?
- Who are the primary and secondary readers?
- What do you know about the reader's situation and how can you address that situation?
- What expectations does the reader bring to the document?
- What format does the reader expect?

Readers' Purpose for the Document

Readers typically will not settle in with a technical document for their reading pleasure. Instead they will seek to locate what they need to know quickly so that they can continue with the task at hand with minimal interruption.

Readers use technical documents for one of three reasons, although sometimes the reader's purpose will cover more than one of these reasons:

- Gathering information
- Completing a task
- Making an informed decision

Using strategies such as visual hierarchies and visual cues to assist readers in locating the data they need will enable them to complete their jobs successfully.

Primary and Secondary Readers

When professional writers create a document, typically they have a specific reader in mind. This reader may be the supervisor who asked for the document or may be a client or customer seeking information. In each case the person to whom you direct the document is its **primary reader**. This primary reader is the person or people who will probably be your first readers and who may be in a position to determine if your writing is useful.

Your primary reader is not your only reader though. Most documents will also have **secondary readers**, or readers who you should reasonably assume will use your document, even if they are not the people who you directly address in your writing. For example, if you are writing instructions for using a particular function in a computer program, you may assume that you are addressing entry-level users who are not especially familiar with your product. Sometimes, though, experienced readers may encounter an issue that leads them to read your instructions for that function. Similarly, if you are providing information about how to access employee benefits through a website, your readers may not only include individuals who work for your organization and are familiar with its jargon, but potentially spouses and partners of employees as well as stakeholders who are invested in the topic but who do not have comprehensive knowledge of the organization and its practices.

Meeting the needs of both primary and secondary readers will help to ensure that your document has the best chance to be successful.

Readers' Situation

An array of elements of your readers' situation will impact their ability and interest in using your document effectively. Each of the qualities detailed below will have a critical impact on the usefulness of your professional documents:

- ***Education level:*** Readers' level of formal education will determine a variety of attributes for your document, including the words you select, the complexity of your sentences, and the amount of jargon that you can safely use. When in doubt choose simple and streamlined language over complicated and dense language.
- ***Background:*** Similar to the readers' education, their background in the general subject will determine how much explanation you should provide. Readers with limited background knowledge of your topic will require more detailed explanations and definitions of terms compared to more advanced readers.
- ***Level of experience:*** In general the amount of experience your readers have in the field and with the specific task in question, as well as their general knowledge of the organization and its expectations, will help you to determine an appropriate level of detail for the document you are creating.

- ***Environment while reading:*** Readers using a document in a traditional office setting will have dramatically different needs than readers in an industrial or factory setting. You may deliver instructions for using a piece of software electronically, whereas instructions for a piece of equipment used in a mechanic's shop may need to be adapted to suit an environment that would be inappropriate for a paper report.
- ***Interest in your material:*** Readers will pay closer attention to information that interests them. That level of interest may derive from a natural inclination toward the subject or it may come from the fact that they'd like to finish the task at hand and move on to something else—or go home for the day. As a result, think in terms of how you can make your message as concise as possible so that your readers can use it efficiently.

What Do Readers Expect of the Document?

Readers who process technical data often have preconceived notions of what a particular type of document should include, how it should be formatted, or even how it should be worded. For example, readers may expect a formal proposal to include front and end matter, such as tables of contents, lists of illustrations and figures, and indices.

A routine correspondence, like a memo or email, would not include these formal elements. A progress report should explain both what has been done on a project so far and what remains to be accomplished, and should include a plan of action to achieve the remaining tasks by the project deadline. Documents that do not include the attributes that readers expect will seldom be deemed complete or acceptable. Knowing the readers' expectations prior to creating a document will assist you, as the writer, in ensuring that you provide everything the reader needs to use your document effectively.

What Format Does the Reader Expect?

In addition to readers' expectations for the content of professional writing, format considerations also play into the creation of documents. A memo should include the expected elements in the header—to, from, date, and subject—but should not include a signature block at the end. Letters, since they are more formal, typically are presented on the company's letterhead that identifies not only the company but its contact information.

Unlike the memo a letter should include a salutation, a signature block, and other conventions of a formal letter. A feasibility study that does not clearly identify the sections readers will expect, complete with appropriate headings, will not likely win the readers' approval. In short, if you present a document in an unfamiliar or inappropriate format, you will undercut your credibility with the reader and minimize the chance for your document to be useful.

ORGANIZATION

Organizing your material in a reasonable manner is critically important to the readers' ability to comprehend and use it. Considering the way that you want to organize your material before you begin to write will help you to develop a final product that will help the readers achieve their goals in using the document.

The **inverted pyramid** organizational strategy places the most important information in front of the reader right way. In an inverted pyramid organizational structure, the writer starts with what journalists call the five Ws and an H: who, what, when, where, why, and how. Present this critical information first, in a clear and concise manner, and then circle back to elaborate on aspects that require additional explanation.

Place the most important aspects of your message front and center, *before* the reader can make a mistake that the inverted pyramid will help them to avoid. If there are steps a reader must take before starting up a piece of equipment, be sure to list them before you ask the reader to turn on the machine. If you need to provide safety warnings, list them in detail before the point in the process when the reader needs to know about them to avoid an accident.

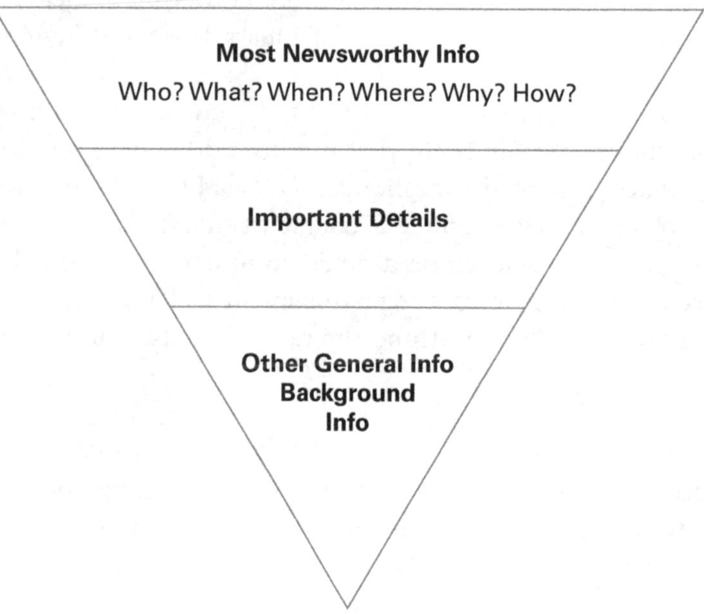

STYLE

Technical writing style should be clear, concise, and get directly to your point with as little extra information or language as possible. Your readers will not be parsing your writing for your beautiful, fluid prose or your expansive vocabulary. They will be seeking specific information, and your job as the writer is to provide that information in as straightforward a manner as you can. Chapter 2 will give you a great deal more information about technical style and how to tailor your writing to the readers' needs.

DESIGN

The design of your documents will be almost as important as the words themselves. If your readers can't locate the information they seek, your document will not be useful. Be sure to consider important design elements, such as chunking text, using a top-down hierarchy, white space, appropriate headings, and visual cues such as color and typography. Chapter 3 will provide an extensive discussion of designing visual texts that will work well for your readers.

CASE STUDIES

Use what you have learned about meeting the needs of the reader in the case studies below.

Case Study 1

You have been in your current job for two years without a salary increase. You decide to discuss this with your supervisor, who agrees that you probably deserve a raise. However, your supervisor isn't the person who can make this decision, so she asks you to write a formal letter requesting a salary bump and making the argument as to why you deserve one. Keeping in mind the needs of the reader, draft the letter that your supervisor has requested.

Case Study 2

You work in the insurance department of a metropolitan hospital. You've been asked to inform all staff members—including doctors, nurses, and technicians, as well as support staff like administrative assistants, housekeeping workers, etc.—about new rules for reporting when someone is injured on the job. Everyone must be informed in writing because of requirements from the hospital's insurance carrier. How will you best get this information out to your readers? What will you say, what form will it take, and how will you deliver it? Remembering that you have readers with many different backgrounds, education levels, and skill sets, write and design the document you will use to communicate this information.

Credits

Fig. 1.1: Source: https://commons.wikimedia.org/wiki/File:Inverted_pyramid.svg.

CHAPTER TWO

Technical Writing Style

Technical style is one of the three fundamental building blocks that lead to effective technical documents. The three building blocks of effective technical communication include:

- Providing for the needs of your readers
- Using a concrete, readable technical style
- Designing documents that are readable, attractive, and easy for readers to use

As you learned in the previous chapter, providing your readers with what they need is the first step to creating useful documents. Technical style focuses on the ways in which you communicate your information so that your readers can easily understand your message, even if the material you are covering is complex or unfamiliar.

Readers of technical documents have different purposes for reading compared to individuals reading for pleasure, so your writing style must help them to find the information that they need. Readers will not find documents useful when they have to search for the key pieces of data that they need to fulfill their purpose for reading. Accordingly, to meet the needs of your readers, you want to adopt a technical style that is:

- **Clear:** Do not make your readers interpret your writing before they can understand your message.
- **Concise:** Get to the point as quickly as possible without adding extraneous commentary or verbiage.
- **Simple:** Use essential, straightforward language and minimize jargon, especially for readers who are not specialists in the field about which you are writing.
- **Direct:** Avoid beating around the bush or building up to your point. State your purpose clearly and succinctly.

- **Concrete:** Choose words that are specific, unambiguous, and relevant to your message.

Technical style operates on three levels, each of which will help to make your message as clear as possible:

- Choosing appropriate words
- Writing concise sentences
- Creating cohesive paragraphs

This chapter will introduce you to the key concepts of each aspect of technical style.

CHOOSING APPROPRIATE WORDS

The words you choose are critical to the clarity of your message. Readers will not find documents effective if they must analyze your language before they can unpack your meaning. Consider the following strategies as you choose words that are appropriate to the needs of your readers.

Select Simple Words Rather than Complex Words

Oftentimes writers feel that they must show off their vocabularies at any opportunity to illustrate that they are well read and well informed. However, high-level vocabulary that the reader must interpret before getting to the point of your message will not serve the readers' needs effectively. Instead select words that are simple and straightforward, allowing the readers to easily locate and comprehend the information they need so that they can move on with the tasks they are trying to complete. Table 2.1 below shows a few examples:

TABLE 2.1 Simple vs Complex Words

INSTEAD OF	TRY
instigate	start
attempt	try
compensate	pay
enhance	improve
facilitate	cause, help
interface	connect
discrepancy	error

TABLE 2.1 continued

INSTEAD OF	TRY
terminate	fire
initiate	begin
capability	ability
initial	first
ascertain	discover

Avoid Varying Terms Unnecessarily

Writers are often encouraged to demonstrate the breadth of their vocabularies when writing for an academic audience. In technical documents, though, using the same terms consistently will minimize confusion for the reader.

Avoid Wasted Words/Phrases

To make your message easier for your reader to digest, look for opportunities to remove words that aren't needed and streamline your sentences. Otherwise your sentence might come across as wordy and hard to follow. A good rule of thumb is to **never use two words when one will do**.

Consider these guidelines to make your writing more straightforward:

- Delete conversational words that intensify but do not add meaning. We use conversational words unconsciously, similar to clearing our throats. Remove these words from your writing:

kind of	actually	really	basically
certain	various	practically	virtually
particular	individual	given	very

Example:

Wordy: Productivity **actually** depends on **certain** factors that **basically** involve psychology more than on any particular technology.

Concise: Productivity depends on psychology more than technology.

- Reduce or delete who, which, and that (relative) clauses

relative clause
The cook *who was flipping hamburgers* had Mom tattooed on his arm.
The cook flipping hamburgers had Mom tattooed on his arm.
relative clause
The salesperson *who sold used cars* starred in the TV commercial.
The used-car salesperson starred in the TV commercial.

- Delete repetitious phrases: each and every, one and all, first and foremost, past history, future plans, sudden crisis
- Delete words/phrases implied by other words

Redundant elements: Words/phrases that repeat the same information. Delete the words in italics in your writing, as illustrated in table 2.3:

TABLE 2.3

advance planning	few *in number*	never *at any time*
and therefore	filled *to capacity*	*original* source
appear *to be*	*final* outcome	*passing* phase
as to whether	*first* priority	*past* history
at an earlier *time*	follow *after*	*pre*plan
attach *together*	smile *on her face*	protrude *out*
basic essentials	gather *together*	return *back*
blue *in color*	graceful *in appearance*	round *in shape*
bright in color	*hot*-water heater	separate *apart*
but nevertheless	inside *of*	*serious* danger
close proximity	*invited* guest	*sink* down
completely finished	join *together*	small *in size*
connect *together*	large *in size*	strangled *to death*
cooperate *together*	*mutual* cooperation	*total* annihilation
eliminate *altogether*	last *of all*	*true* facts
end product	lift *up*	*violent* explosion
end result	*local* resident	worthy *of merit*
fellow colleagues	may *possibly*	3 p.m. *in the afternoon*

Redundant Modifiers: Often the meaning of a word implies its modifier, as table 2.4 shows:

TABLE 2.4

terrible tragedy	various different	free gift
basic fundamentals	future plans	each individual
final outcome	true facts	consensus of opinion

Redundant categories: Restating concrete words in the abstract. The abstraction puts the concrete word into a category and distracts the reader from what your writing is trying to convey, as table 2.5 shows:

TABLE 2.5

shiny *in appearance*	period *of time*	honest *in character*
large *in size*	round *in shape*	*at an* earlier *time*
unusual *in nature*	*of a* strange *type*	a career in *the medical profession*
red *in color*	*upright* position	time *period*

Remember—never use two words when one will do.

Correcting Redundancies

You may have to change an adjective into an adverb.

Incorrect: The holes must be aligned in an accurate manner.
Correct: The holes must be aligned accurately.

You may have to change an adjective into a noun.

Incorrect: The county is responsible for the educational system and public recreational activities.
Correct: The county is responsible for education and public recreation.

- Replace a phrase with a word, as table 2.6 shows:

TABLE 2.6

PHRASES	REPLACE WITH
at present	now
by means of	by
despite the fact that	although, even though, despite
due to the fact that	because
for the purpose of	for
in order to	to
in spite of the fact that	although, even though, despite
in the event that	if
owing to the fact that	because
so as to	to
the fact that	that
this is why	why

- Avoid vague, abstract words and phrases as table 2.7 shows:

TABLE 2.7

many	often	soon
frequently	many	a small amount of
rarely	a majority of	lots
a lot	not many	a little
few	several	a variety of
some	a number of	a great deal of
numerous	most	

- Avoid vague, throwaway intensifiers such as table 2.8 shows

TABLE 2.8

very	extremely	really
generally	basically	somewhat
fairly		

- Avoid wordy phrases that make you seem unsure

  Writers often try to use these words to make themselves sound more confident. In addition to delaying the actor and action, these words actually make the writer seem unsure. This type of sentence construction moves the actual actor and action to the end of the sentence, as table 2.9 shows:

TABLE 2.9

I think (that)	In my opinion
I feel (that)	It seems (to me) (that)
I believe (that)	It appears (that)
It is evident (that)	

- Write in the affirmative rather than the negative. Select a concise word that describes your idea instead of using a negative phrase.

  As table 2.10 shows, when you express an idea in a negative form, not only do you have to use an extra word (same–not different), but you also force your readers to do some type of algebraic factoring.

TABLE 2.10

not different–similar	not many–few
not the same–different	not often–rarely
not allow–prevent	not stop–continue
not notice–overlook	not include–omit

- Use verb tense rather than extra words or phrases. Below, table 2.11 provides examples:

TABLE 2.11

currently	at present	in the past
in the future	presently	

Use Action Verbs/Avoid Overusing "To Be" Verbs

As you learned in the previous chapter, the reader often uses your technical documents to complete a task or make a decision. In other words readers will likely refer to your document as they work through a task or process. Using action verbs will assist the readers in completing the workload.

Writers frequently rely on forms of the verb "to be" as the primary verb in their sentences, but these (static) verbs do not communicate the action that a reader took or the event that transpired. Revising sentences to remove forms of "to be" in favor of more active verbs will make your message more concise for readers:

- Be verb: The meeting was long and boring
- **Action verb:** The long, boring meeting did not follow the agenda.
- Be verb: Everyone was ready to go long before the meeting ended.
- **Action verb:** As soon as the meeting ended, everyone marched toward the exits.

Use Concrete Nouns

In conjunction with using active verbs, select concrete nouns over vague, abstract ones. The more specific your word choices, the clearer your message is to your reader.

Readers identify concrete nouns because they are perceived through one or more of the five senses (i.e.: taste, sight, hearing, touch, or smell). Abstract nouns are not perceived through the senses and often encompass concepts and ideas ranging from courage, bravery, or stupidity to corporate culture or work-life balance.

- Abstract: Higher education is necessary for a professional career.
  Concrete: Mohammed attended **college** because he wanted to be an engineer.
- Abstract: It is hard to imagine the courage it takes to be a soldier.
- **Concrete:** Soldiers like Chris Kyle demonstrate both **physical and mental strength** through their service.

Capitalize Only When Necessary

Capitalized letters will grab your readers' attention but only use them when capitalizing is grammatically correct. When you overuse capital letters they lose their effectiveness as a means of emphasizing important information. The exponential growth of the internet has led us to read a great deal of inaccurate and ungrammatical information, and one of the results of this is that we have developed a tendency to capitalize random words just because we can. Grammatical errors result when writers capitalize common nouns and adjectives. If a word is not a proper noun or adjective—the name of a specific person or entity, for example—you should not capitalize it. In addition, if you are still unsure, check the specific style guide you plan on using for your writing.

Choose Gender-Neutral Terms

Traditionally readers accepted gender-biased language because it represented normative language use. However, you will alienate many of your readers—and not just female readers—if you choose to use language that suggests that all readers of a particular type belong to one gender.

In contemporary America some readers will not consider gender to be binary—that is to say that not everyone is either male or female. As a result you may encounter some readers whose preference is to be referred to using the plural they rather than the gender-specific he/she or him/her. For example, if a reader prefers to be referenced as they instead of he/she, strive to accommodate the reader's desire. Alternately some readers may be put off by this type of language use. In all situations keep the readers' needs in mind, and strive to meet those needs without allowing personal politics or beliefs to drive your word choices. Readers tend to hold such positions strongly, and alienating these readers will not lead to successful communication.

Consider these guidelines when writing for readers of diverse genders.

Use gender-neutral terms

Rather than using terms that include an implicit gender, select words that do not specify gender. For examples refer to table 2.12:

TABLE 2.12

INSTEAD OF	TRY
Chairman	Chair or chairperson
Policeman	Officer or police officer
Mankind	Humankind, humanity, people
Man-made	Synthetic, manufactured
Man the front desk	Staff the front desk

Refer to individuals of different genders in parallel terms

When women began to enter the workforce in large numbers during and after World War 2, workplace language often indicated a hierarchy that placed men at a higher level than women. One indicator of this hierarchy was a tendency to address men by their title and last name—Mr. James or Dr. Brown—but to refer to women by their first names. This practice has fallen far out of favor; you should refer to all individuals in a similar manner:

- Biased: Mr. Smith and Jane attended the sales conference.
- **Unbiased:** Mr. Smith and Ms. Jones attended the sales conference.
- **Unbiased:** Joe and Jane attended the sales conference.
- Biased: Dr. Brown and Marcus wrote the prospectus and presented it to the board.
- **Unbiased:** Drs. Brown and Evans wrote the prospectus and presented it to the board.
- **Unbiased:** Maria and Marcus wrote the prospectus and presented it to the board.

WRITING CONCISE SENTENCES

Readers bring unspoken expectations to anything they read, and these expectations are based on a lifetime of experience reading widely varied documents. Presenting your information in a style that is comfortable and customary to your readers will ensure that your message comes across clearly. Typically readers will (subconsciously) expect two things:

- The central character or concept you are discussing appears as the subject of the sentence. Make actors the subjects of sentences.
- The most important action(s) of those subjects are communicated through verbs.

Use Human Subjects

Whenever possible try to make people the subjects of your sentences. When you write sentences without people as subjects, your writing will sound abstract or impersonal and bureaucratic.

People aren't subjects

As announced earlier, the prescription drug card program will be eliminated effective at the end of the year. Effective January 1, prescriptions that are purchased from local pharmacies may be filled and will be paid at 80% after a $200 deductible. This means that all prescriptions purchased from local pharmacies must be paid for and the receipts saved. A claim form and your receipts should then be mailed in for reimbursement.

People are subjects

As announced earlier, **you** will begin using a new prescription drug program on January 1. Instead of using your prescription drug card, **you** may file with us any prescriptions **you** purchase from local pharmacies. **We** will pay 80% of the cost of your prescriptions after you meet the $200 deductible. To take advantage of this new program, **(you)** follow four simple steps:

> Pay for all prescriptions purchased at local pharmacies.
> Save the receipts.
> Complete the attached form.
> Mail the completed form in the envelope provided, so we can reimburse you.

Expletive Constructions

An expletive construction is an expression that occupies the subject position of a sentence or clause. The two common expletives are **it** and **there** followed by a form of the verb "to be."

- **It is** true that Luigi missed the party. (It occupies the position of the subject, but the real subject is the clause that Luigi missed the party.)
- **There are** twenty-six letters in the English alphabet. (There occupies the position of subject, but the real subject is letters.)

Expletives, while grammatically correct, are often unnecessary and create wordy sentences. An expletive inverts the usual order of subject and verb.

> Incorrect: There is a case of meningitis that was reported in the newspaper.
> **Correct:** The newspaper reported a case of meningitis. (Active voice)

Incorrect: It is important to signal before making a left turn.
Correct: Always signal before making a left turn. (Active Voice)

Incorrect: There are some revisions which must be made.
Correct: Please revise your documents for the following problems:

- Passive voice
- Nominalizations
- Expletive constructions

Correcting expletive constructions

To correct expletive constructions, simply remove the **it** or **there** and the **"to be" verb** and begin the sentence with the appropriate subject.

We lost
~~There were~~ many orders lost for some unexplained reason.

He certainly
~~It is certain~~ that he will go.

Use Active Voice

When you use passive voice, readers must search for actors or infer their identity. When you use active voice, the actor is the grammatical subject, as readers expect.

Passive voice occurs when the verb consists of an auxiliary (helping) verb that is a form of the verb "to be":

am, is, are, was, were, be, being, been

The "to be" verb (supports) a verb in the past participle. A past participle is the form of a verb that requires an auxiliary verb. Below, table 2.13 provides specific examples:

TABLE 2.13

PRESENT	PAST	PAST PARTICIPLE
Jump	Jumped	Jumped
Listen	Listened	Listened
Run	Ran	Run
Sing	Sang	Sung

When a form of "to be" joins with a past participle, the result is a sentence in the passive voice. Readers will have to search for the intended meaning of the statement.

Changing from passive to active voice
To revise your sentence from passive to active voice, follow these steps:

1. Identify the actor in the sentence. What/who is the actual subject being discussed?
2. Make the actor the subject of the sentence
3. Follow the actor with the action of the sentence. Use an active verb.

Passive Voice: As announced earlier, the prescription drug card program will be eliminated effective at the end of the year.
Active Voice: As announced earlier, we **will eliminate** the prescription drug card program at the end of the year.

Passive Voice: The solar eclipse was observed by all of the members of the astronomy class.
Active Voice: All members of the astronomy class observed the solar eclipse.

Avoid Nominalizations

Readers expect to find the action in a sentence residing in the verb—the grammatical source of action. Sometimes writers nominalize a verb, turning it into a noun and then using a weaker, less exact verb to replace it. You can inadvertently nominalize adjectives as well. Nominalizing verbs or adjectives will dilute your message and may confuse your reader. In short, sentences that use nominalizations may be hard to follow.

Nominalizations occur when a verb has a suffix added to the end, turning it into a noun. Common suffixes include:

-tion, -ment, -en, -ce, -y, -ation, -an, -s/is

Examples of nominalizations are shown in table 2.14. They include terms like:

TABLE 2.14

VERB	NOMINALIZATION
Inform	Information
Situate	Situation
Proceed	Procedure
Suggest	Suggestion
Analyze	Analysis
Collect	Collection
Investigate	Investigation
Decide	Decision
Fly	Flying
Resist	Resistance

Your sentences will be clearest when you use verbs as they are intended—to communicate the action taking place in your sentences. Consider the clarity of the examples below:

- Nominalization: It was suggested that an investigation be initiated to determine if the company made fraudulent transactions.
- **Active verb:** The board suggested that we investigate whether fraud had occurred.
- Nominalization: The FBI conducted a complete investigation of the director's claims.
- **Active verb:** The FBI **investigated** the director's claims.
- Nominalization: The intention of the administration was to obscure the records behind an IRS audit.
- **Active verb:** The administrators **claimed** they could not release the records because of an IRS audit.

"Empty" Verbs

Nominalized verbs often depend upon other words to carry the action of the sentence. The italicized words below indicate the "empty" verbs. When you revise your technical documents for nominalizations, you will be able to delete these "empty" verbs, thereby making a more concise and verbal sentence.

provide an explanation	~~provide an~~ explanation	explain
came to a conclusion	~~came to a~~ conclusion	concluded
reach a decision	~~reach a~~ decision	decide
provide or *offer* support	~~provide or offer~~ support	support
had the belief that	~~had the~~ belief that	believed

STYLE ACTIVITY

Watch Helen Sword's Ted Talks video "Beware of nominalizations (AKA zombie nouns)" (https://youtu.be/dNlkHtMgcPQf).

Once you've watched the video, answer the following questions. Be prepared to discuss your answers in class.

1. Why do you think Helen Sword calls them "zombie nouns"?
2. Which of the following is a possible suffix you can add to a verb or adjective to make a nominalization?
   A. -ance
   B. -ation
   C. -ism
   D. all of the above
3. Who typically uses nominalizations in their writing?
   A. academics
   B. lawyers
   C. business writers
   D. all of the above
4. Which of the following is NOT a nominalization?
   A. approach
   B. comparison
   C. clear
   D. increase

Use Lists to Emphasize

Readers typically skim technical documents searching for specific pieces of data that they need. They may use a document while they are actively completing a task because your document shows them how. Your readers will find it helpful if you present lists and step-by-step instructions as either bulleted or numerical lists. Lists stand out on a page and draw readers' attention. If readers are following a set of steps you have laid out, finding their place in the process is easier in a list than in a paragraph.

Create Parallel Structures

Parallel structure means using the same pattern of words to show that two or more ideas have the same level of importance. This can happen at the word, phrase, or clause level. The usual way to join parallel structures is by using coordinating conjunctions such as and, but, and or.

For lists to be accurate, they should be grammatically parallel. Each item in a list should begin with the same part of speech—ideally, with a verb.

> Not Parallel: Mary likes hiking, swimming, and to ride a bicycle.
> **Parallel:** Mary likes hiking, swimming, and riding a bicycle.
>
> Not Parallel: The production manager was asked to write his report quickly, accurately, and in a detailed manner.
> **Parallel:** The production manager was asked to write his report quickly, accurately, and thoroughly.
>
> Not Parallel: The teacher said that he was a poor student because he waited until the last minute to study for the exam, completed his lab problems in a careless manner, and his motivation was low.
> **Parallel:** The teacher said that he was a poor student because he waited until the last minute to study for the exam, completed his lab problems in a careless manner, and lacked motivation.

Emphasize Important Information in Sentences

You can convey your intended message and help readers understand your documents quickly if you emphasize the important information in your sentences. You can do this in two ways:

1. Put important information at the end of the sentence.
2. Put unfamiliar and technical terms at the end of the sentence.

Put the Most Important Information at the End

The natural stress point of most sentences is the end. When reading a sentence aloud, you tend to raise the pitch of your voice near the end and stress the last few words. When writing you can take advantage of this natural stress point to emphasize important information.

Examples:

Less important appears in *italics*, the more important in **bold**.
You have not sent us **your December progress report**, *according to our records.*
The profits in January **increased by 30 percent**, *for example.*

In both of these sentences, unimportant prepositional phrases appear at the end. By moving these phrases to the beginning of the sentence, the writer emphasizes the more important information about the progress report and increase in profits.

According to our records, you have not mailed **your December progress report**.
For example, the profits in January **increased by 30 percent.**

Put unfamiliar technical terms at the end

Readers better understand unfamiliar information if you put it at the end of sentences. If you put it near the beginning, readers don't have the context clues for understanding unfamiliar information.

Example:

Fast-twitch fibers and *slow-twitch fibers* are the two basic types of muscle fibers.
Muscles have two types of fibers: *fast twitch and slow twitch.*

By putting the familiar "muscles" at the beginning of the sentence, the writer gives the readers a context for the unfamiliar "fast twitch" and "slow twitch."

Place Key Information in the Main Clause of a Sentence

If your sentence contains more than one clause, use the main clause to convey the information you want to emphasize.

Although our tuition went up, our **enrollment increased**.
Although our enrollment increased, our **tuition rose** significantly.

In each statement, the bold text is the idea emphasized in the sentence. You can choose to use visual cues like bold or italic type to emphasize important ideas, although you should do so sparingly. Lots of visual cues render them all ineffective, because they are distracting or may overwhelm the reader.

Avoid Sentences with Multiple Clauses

Readers typically prefer sentences that consist of one clause rather than several, as these sentences are easier to comprehend. Rather than stringing together several clauses into one sentence, creating compound, complex, or compound-complex sentences, strive to present each idea in one concise statement. Move on to another sentence when you begin another idea. For example:

- **Compound sentence:** The meeting began at noon, but the speaker did not begin his talk until nearly 2:00; everyone became uncomfortable after sitting so long without a break.
- **Simple sentences:** The meeting began at noon. The speaker did not begin his talk until nearly 2:00. Everyone became uncomfortable after sitting so long without a break.

CREATING COHESIVE PARAGRAPHS

Write in Short Paragraphs, or Chunk Text

Readers often skim technical documents rather than reading them word-for-word. Long paragraphs may hide the information readers are seeking. Breaking your thoughts into smaller segments will facilitate skimming, allowing readers to locate the information they need to continue with their work.

By breaking ideas into shorter paragraphs, or smaller chunks, and combining this strategy with visual cues and lists, you can assist readers in locating what they need to know. You will also break the monotony of huge paragraphs and allow readers to find the parts of the document that they find important.

Favor Short Sentences Over Long, Complex Ones

Sentences in English typically follow this pattern to form an **independent clause**, or a sentence that can stand on its own and be complete:

- Subject **> Verb > Object**
- The dog caught the ball.
- The vice president appointed a new manager for our department.
- The design of the document helped the reader follow the process.

These examples each use one independent clause to state the point clearly. They also begin with human subjects or concrete concepts that are followed by a strong, action verb. The reader can easily determine the meaning of the statement without a great deal of processing.

Often multiple clauses may be put together to vary the flow of a paragraph in an academic paper or in a creative work. However, more complicated sentence structure may cause the reader to struggle to follow the logic and connection between the statements. In the interest of allowing your readers to easily parse your message, write shorter sentences that follow the subject > verb > object pattern.

Use Details Wisely

Deciding how extensive the details you provide on a topic need to be is a bit like walking on a tightrope. As writers, we often want to give the reader everything we possibly can about a topic that we know a great deal about. However, readers want only enough detail to understand the topic or complete their task. To meet the needs of your readers, balance detail with the audience's need for clarity and concision. Ask yourself if details you wish to include are significant to readers' purpose.

Strive for a Natural Sound

While academic writing discourages writers from using a conversational style, readers of technical documents will appreciate reading material that does not challenge their ability to comprehend it. Work toward writing to readers as if you are talking to them and walking them through the processes while they complete them.

Think Visually to Reduce Text

Finally, consider ways in which you can present your information visually and minimize the amount of text your readers must process.

Provide Visual Structure to Documents

Human subject

1. To sign up for the class, have a photo ID ready.
2. Before taking out the flash drive, make sure to eject it.
3. Do not take more than one pill every eight hours.
4. Submit the assignment before 12:59 pm.
5. When signing up for season tickets, be sure to fill out the entire registration form.
6. Before changing a tire, make sure to loosen the lug nuts.
7. Have questions? Please use a student ID number to login and chat with us.
8. Have the group write an email discussing the problems.

9. Loans must be paid in full by December.
10. The baseball all-star game is around the corner. Select the Rangers before it's too late!

Passive voice

The group assignment was completed by one person.
The students were really trying to enhance their grades by asking for extra credit.
We were being silly while trying to work.
The class was being very loud because they had just come in from recess.
On Friday, she is going to be celebrating turning in her portfolio.
We will be throwing a party on Saturday.
In spite of the fact that the meeting was running late, we were still able to attend dinner.
We were attempting to pack, but the sad news story on TV interfered.
She was trying to concentrate in the loud coffee shop.
Are you going to be able to attend City Council meetings in the future?

Nominalization

1. The investigation lasted for a long time.
2. The distortion caused the band to sound really bad.
3. Our intervention for her son proved unsuccessful.
4. The expansion of the pipes happened because of the cold weather.
5. The information written on the syllabus was incorrect.
6. The line backer's interference caused the team to lose.
7. The resistance ended with a happy resolution.
8. If you have any suggestions, please feel free to email us.
9. The procedure lasts two hours.
10. Discrimination will not be tolerated.

Select simple words rather than complex

1. The judge facilitated the meeting to make sure all sides were heard.
2. To dispute the discrepancy, we took the assignment to the teacher.

3. Effective immediately, we need to terminate your job.
4. She instigated a fight to avoid having to work.
5. By enhancing the document's readability, you help your audience find the content he or she needs.

Avoid wasted words/phrases

1. We basically completed the project all in one night.
2. She sang very loudly in the shower.
3. The baseball player who was at home plate hit a homerun.
4. First and foremost, you will write a bio about yourself.
5. The teacher who talks loudly wants to offer extra credit for the upcoming assignment.

Redundant elements

1. She is graceful in appearance, but in reality, she trips over everything.
2. Not many people watched the final outcome of the game.
3. Our future plans did not happen because of the hurricane.
4. Many people considered Abe Lincoln honest in character.
5. Due to the fact that the train was late, we missed our flight.

Use action verbs/avoid overusing "to be" verbs

1. She did not allow herself enough time to get to work. She was very late.
2. Darlene is being taken to the vet because of fleas.
3. As described on the syllabus, the paper will be due on October 6th.
4. Everyone will be needed in order for an extremely successful meeting.
5. She is trying to be motivated.

Use concrete nouns

1. Her happiness brightened up the room.
2. The millennial generation tends to buy homes later in life.
3. Mother Teresa's compassion helped many people.
4. Thank you to the national guard for their bravery.
5. Albert Einstein's brilliance lead to the discovery of the formula $E = mc^2$

Capitalize only when necessary

1. The House of Representatives will try to pass the Bill.
2. She likes to study Archeology.
3. The Mayor proposed budget cuts.
4. To get to Denton, take i35 North.
5. My brother's girlfriend is laotian.

Choose gender-neutral terms

During this meeting, we will pick a new chairman.
Over time, man-made structures such as the Eiffel Tower will need major repairs.
In order to reduce police–civilian violence, the policemen participate in training.
The waitress spilled her tray.
Mr. White and Sarah are unhappy with their new house decor.

Expletive constructions

1. There are many reasons for the earthquake.
2. There are several decisions we need to make before our trip to Costa Rica.
3. There is only room enough for one of us.
4. There are long nights ahead of us.
5. It is important to turn off all the lights before leaving the house.

Create parallel structures

1. When not a work, Silva likes to run, hiking, and swimming.
2. Tony enjoys going to the beach, outdoor running, and family vacations.
3. The hot days not only mean enjoying the pool but also to eat bbq and to drink ice cold lemonade.
4. The student decided to take classes in math, geography, political science, and studying psychology.
5. He needs to work quick and decisively.

Emphasize important information in sentences

1. We cannot wait until tomorrow night because the rent is due sooner.
2. We are donating supplies to the Red Cross and it's due later tomorrow evening.
3. You have not submitted your payment to financial aid, according to our records.
4. Your stock went up by 15% last February.
5. Don't forget to submit your assignment by midnight or I will deduct a letter grade.

Put unfamiliar technical terms at the end

The cryosphere is the frozen water layer of the Earth.
Cryptology helps protect digital data.
Intellectual property is considered intangible. It often refers to things such as ideas, names, designs, symbols, artwork, writings, and other creations.
I study ethnomusicology. My specialty includes blues music from the Mississippi Delta.
SEO Keywords help Google find your website.

Place key information in the main clause of a sentence

1. You require eight hours of sleep to function normally.
2. Teachers need to submit their grades by midnight.
3. You must keep running in order to lose weight.
4. Rewrite the sentences or you're fired.
5. Correct this error unless you want a bad grade.

Avoid sentences with multiple clauses

1. Edgar Allan Poe loved animals, but later died from rabies after a long night of drinking; his books include many animal themes.
2. Many people find Tina Fey funny, and her SNL skits are often laugh out loud, so is her show 30 Rock.
3. Heavy metal incorporates many classical music elements, and often people who listen to it are considered to have higher IQs because of the intricacies.
4. Beagles are part of the Canidae family, and they love to bark and howl at squirrels while running madly around the yard.

5. Stevie Ray Vaughn is often known as the King of Texas music, but many argue Lead Belly or Lightnin' Hopkins holds the title.

Creating cohesive paragraphs
Example 1

Dear Mr. Jones and Martha,
Hockey season is about to start soon. Registration for season tickets will be available in August. We are extremely excited to welcome many people back. As always, we will not stop attempting to provide the best service possible. Sign up now to receive a free gift from us.
See you soon!

Example 2

Dear chairman,
I am writing to you because I am upset about the new red-light camera at St. Paul street. It is located North of the church and South of I35. Although you seem to think it was effective, people have been having accidents still. I have witnessed an accident nearly every single day because my office is located right across the way.
Please tell me the end results of your decision, and whether or not you will try to resolve this very dangerous issue.
If you need additional information, please do not hesitate to call me.

Thank You,

Mr. Pink

CHAPTER THREE

Designing and Formatting Visual Texts

One of the foundational elements of effective technical communication is designing visual texts that present readable, easily comprehended technical information. This is one of the main areas where technical writers often fail.

TYPOGRAPHY

You aid your readers' understanding by using the most appropriate font. To avoid visual conflict many designers avoid using two fonts of the same family, such as two serif fonts.

Monospaced versus Proportional

Fonts on typewriters were usually monospaced (mono—one space). Monospaced means that all characters take up exactly the same amount of space, regardless of whether the character is a capital M or a lowercase i.

	MONOSPACED	PROPORTIONALLY SPACED
Proportionally spaced fonts are kerned.	Mi	Mi

Unlike typewriters, today most of the digital typefaces used on computers are designed to be proportionally spaced. With proportionally spaced typefaces, characters have just the necessary amount of space between them. With a proportional font, you can fit more text on a page as well as increase legibility by avoiding design problems such as rivers of white, which are large white gaps between characters created by a word-processing program attempting to align text on both the right and left margins.

10PT. MONOSPACED FONT WITH FULL JUSTIFICATION AND RIVERS OF WHITE	10 PT. PROPORTIONALLY SPACED FONT WITH RAGGED RIGHT JUSTIFICATION
With a proportional font, you can fit more text on a page, as well as increase legibility by avoiding design problems such as rivers of white.	With a proportional font, you can fit more text on a page, as well as increase legibility by avoiding design problems such as rivers of white.

Always use a serif font in the body text of paper documents. Serif fonts guide the reader's eye across the page, which is suitable for dense text blocks. Use a suitable sans serif typeface for titles, headings, and subheadings, design elements that readers skim and scan to find the information they need.

	FONT FAMILIES	BEST USED WITH	DON'T USE WITH
T	**Serif** fonts have contrasting strokes and lines.	**Print text blocks** Help move reader's eye from character to character. Font family most readers are familiar with.	**Small point sizes** **Digital texts** **Reverse text** Make words appear blurry.
T	**Sans serif** fonts have uniform strokes throughout. Sans serif typefaces have more contrast than serif typefaces.	**Titles** **Headings and subheadings** **Small point sizes** **Digital text** **Reverse text** Help readers easily read text.	**Text blocks** Make words in a sentence hard to follow.

Emphasis

Emphasis means putting stress on a word or a group of words to give it more importance.

Using color for emphasis

Color can be extremely helpful when creating emphasis in visual texts. Color doesn't necessary mean reds, blues, or greens. Black and white are colors too. Emphasis can be accorded to how bold or how large a piece of text is as well as how much black is used against a white or light background.

Using type size for emphasis

Type size indicates the point size of the words: the greater the number of point size, the larger the words and the greater the emphasis.

More Emphasis   Less Emphasis

Using underlining for emphasis

Underlining blocks the descenders in words, the parts of the letter that descend below the line. To prevent this problem, use italics rather than underlining for emphasis in print or digital publications. Reserve underlining strictly for hyperlinks in digital texts.

DESIGN PROBLEM	SERIF	SANS SERIF
Underlining blocks the descenders, the parts of the letter that descend below the line.	pqjy	pqjy

Using all uppercase for emphasis

Readers recognize words by their shape. All uppercase words lack visual distinction, making them more difficult to recognize. Avoid using all uppercase words for emphasis in five or more successive words and then only with sizes of 11 point or greater. Limit uppercase words to titles, headings, and subheadings, which should always be five or fewer words.

DESIGN PROBLEM	ALL UPPERCASE	UPPER AND LOWER-CASE
All uppercase words have no visual distinction.	READERS	Readers
	READERS RECOGNIZE WORDS BYTHEIR SHAPE	Readers recognize words by their shape.

FOCAL POINTS

Contrast

Contrast is what helps guide the readers' eyes to the most important parts of your design and helps organize the information in an easily discernable manner. Contrast is the difference between elements (text or background) such that the combination of those elements makes one element stand out from another.

Texts—digital or print—display the same range of contrast. When we look at a field of text, we rely upon figure–ground contrast to decipher and understand it. The print that we read depends upon typefaces being distinct from the background. When we look at a page or screen, we look for variations across the entire visual field.

In the first example nothing stands out, and you have nothing to focus upon, nothing to guide you visually. For this reason most screens (and pages) have visual variety: paragraph breaks, graphic elements, icons, and illustrations to create contrast. Notice how the pages draw you to certain elements by defining them against a background. Once readers have focal points, they can begin exploring the contents.

Dam Arumquibus

Sed quunt faci odiciatia con re sita velloribus con et doloris ad quiat re, tem que pre parum ilit, sunt alit, inusam el et, volestrum fugit ratem faccabo. Itatempe volut a nulparum eossus, susandigent ut ilia con nonsequi totam eume dolupta cum faccus ent, cusapie nducienis il id eaqui doluptius, si dolorpor atio offic toris repudic to tem quat eatquia vel mo ilignimi, cone as nulpa quod minciis rem nonsene serspid quam velest ut adicips usantios aliquo modis ex essequamet voluptur arum que ese conet qui autemporem res expellenis event apit vitiorr uptur?

Lorempo rpore, nos aut ex eati ipsum qui ium idero maximoditiis aut optataque voluptat volorpor antis es est, que niscit anto invelen delenda ipsapis volluptur as magnihicit apereius autem fuga. Ma con corepud aepeliant.

Vit lacerib usaeptat accum nient laccumq uatiusa percim adi sum ipiet quam recus et doluptatur maionsequid eosam endignata volorpo rempelesto et maximus, omnihil idempelecto in ratur? Qui iduntiu ntempor posanduciet, sum et quam, ium que esequi rehenimint porum, et hiciis eseque si bea volorio. Uptam voloritis mos aliquidel molorpore issimusdam quas rem volupta tisquas cum

Text without Focal Points

Dam Arumquibus

Dam arumquibus

Sed quunt faci odiciatia con re sita velloribus con et doloris ad quiat re, tem que pre parum ilit, sunt alit, inusam el et, volestrum fugit ratem faccabo. Itatempe volut a nulparum si

Dam arumquibus

dolorpor atio offic toris repudic to tem quat eatquia vel mo ilignimi, cone as nulpa quod:

- Minciis rem
- Nonsene serspid
- Quam velest ut

Adicips usantios aliquo modis ex essequamet voluptur arum que ese conet qui autemporem res expellenis.

Text with Focal Points

Page with Focal Points

Bold 12 pt. Sans Serif Heading 1

In presentational writing, you should try to minimize elaboration. One effective method to minimize elaboration is through bulleted lists. When using lists, you should have no more than seven elements.

Another method to aid your readers' understanding is in choosing the most appropriate font. Always use a serif font in the body text of paper documents. Serif fonts guide the reader's eye across the page.

Roman 11 pt. Sans Serif Heading 2 (left-aligned with text)

The following run-in headings allow your readers to assimilate information at a glance:

- **Paragraphs** - Your paragraphs should have no more than 35 words and no more than three sentences. Bolding key words, phrases, or sentences allows you to provide additional schemata by providing your reader with a visual overview.
- **Sentences** - Your sentences should have no more than 17 words. Your point should always be obvious to the reader.
- **Visual Elements** - Paper documentation typically employs listings, headings, subheadings, sectional overviews, and textual introductions and captioning for visual elements. Additional elements such as ragged-right margins can increase your readers' comprehension by 10 percent.

Bold 12 pt. Sans Serif Heading 1

The following visual shows additional methods to design information:

Avoid ALL UPPERCASE WORDS

Xroviderem quam eos que a vollend aepella borum, enis evendio core pro mo doluptat et cum nonectota seque reris doloribusam ullaut evel ium quid ut quam dolupid modit a paruptatet velliquo

Avoid Underlining

Ucit, voloreni bea doluptatiam qui dollige nempernam apit velitat volendit, con exceat repre nemolupid quisite essit quae. Itati aut qui blaborem qui reristium elignatiant eosamusa niscit lat et et ipide liqui quo

Avoid Centered Headings

Doluptatiam qui dollige nempernam apit velitat volendit, con exceat repre nemolupid quisite essit quae. Itati aut qui blaborem qui reristium elignatiant eosamusa niscit lat et et ipide liqui quo volupta quaectur

Avoid full justification

Eque ditet latur ratquos excearchit dit, odipsum sera ipitem hit lam, volestis sum quia ducilitaepe mos enditem faccus doluptaquos adipsanda dolupta conem nonse dolorestibus adit most que con rem. rem dolorup tatqui qui adipsum, eum natianti quasi ommo ommos el int ex eos eles nem exerundia et ex nem.

Avoid text without focal points

Hendele nitiis auditaqui tores denda es dolum ipid eatet hil ipidit modi odipis diquia pliquo beri cumqui arcientiam nuscid ut liquiam quatur, ommodis maximolore endel is dolut quas

All visuals need a caption/heading callout

VISUAL QUEUING

Visual hierarchy helps your audience easily distinguish the levels of importance of information. This hierarchy is called "visual queuing," and you can accomplish it in a variety of ways: using larger or bolder fonts; placing your most important information against the left margin and moving less important information progressively to the right; capitalizing words in captions, headings, and subheadings; and effectively choosing color.

When you design for visual hierarchy, first determine the most important elements on a page or interface. Creating an outline is the easiest way to do this. For example, in a traditional outline, the first-level Roman numeral heading "I" is more important than the second-level capital letter, and the third-level Arabic-numbered heading "1."

I. Executive Summary
II. Introduction
III. The Problem of Where to Live
IV. The Problem of Where to Eat
V. Methods of Research
    A. Questionnaires
    B. Surveys
VI. Results
    A. Residence Halls
    B. On-campus Apartments
    C. Off-campus Apartments
    D. Off-campus Houses
VII. Conclusions & Recommendations
VIII. Appendix A: Survey Questionnaire

First level heading

Ut et plant arionse quatur sus. Nem conse por molupta sperrumquam hil mos rerum la aditis nonsed que velitae pa asi tem accupta tionseque aut.

Second Level Heading

Dundis eum esciusaest exerspera qui doloriae peres sunt. dis aliquam, sa verspel enistest id que nis ipid quidestes non natem niscimi ntiati desed quam, tenditatis est arum sed quam.

First level heading

Itateni mporis aceruptation enimagnis maxim ut evendi occus acest endelle stotaecearit utatios simusan dipsant eaquaepudam reium quam illate con cullatiis es con.

Second Level Heading

Verum vitate dio voloresti dolecea temperchil id minctem velit et del eatur, aut aut aut qui dit qui occus, volupta di reheniae ad quate pra.

Examples of Visual Queuing

Examples of Visual Queuing

Similar to an outline, on a page, screen, or interface, you indicate more important information with a larger type size or boldface type. In addition, similar to the color-coded numbering system in the outline, you can use color as another means to indicate visual hierarchy. Yet another method of visual queuing is alignment. Designers put more important information closer to the left margin and indent successively less important information.

Visual Hierarchy

You have a variety of ways to indicate visual hierarchy in a technical document.

VISUAL HIERARCHY

Contrast	Create contrast by using a serif font for body text and a sans serif font for headings. You can also use italics, bold, or color to create contrast.
Typeface	Use typography to guide readers through the levels of your document.
Type size	Type size indicates the point size of the words. The greater the point size, the larger the words and the greater the importance. **More Important** Less Important
Typestyle	Typestyle indicates the visual distinction of the words: Roman **Bold** *Italic*
Color	Use darker shades of a color for more important textual elements such as titles headings. Then lighten the shades for progressively less important information such as headings, captions, and information in headers and footers.
Alignment	When laying out a document using visual queuing, align the most important information against the left margin, then progressively indent to the right, similar to an outline.

Contrast

Contrast is the difference between elements (text or background) such that the combination of those elements makes one element stand out from another. Contrast is designing documents to distinguish different types of information with different typefaces. One element of contrast is hierarchy—making sure the audience understands that information has different levels of importance.

You can create contrast in a number of ways:

- Color
- Size
- Placement
- Shape
- Content

For example, these three images all show the same word but with different typefaces, colors, and backgrounds.

How do they contrast?

Which is the most effective?

Technology

Which is the most legible?

To aid legibility, consider adding a gradient background behind text, especially if your text color is at all similar to background colors.

COGNITIVE SCAFFOLDING

In designing a page, you should create visuals patterns that help your readers to find, understand, and remember information.

Filtering

Filtering is the use of visual patterns to distinguish various types of information. Repeating visual elements focuses your reader's attention on the information, thus making it easier to understand complex, technical information.

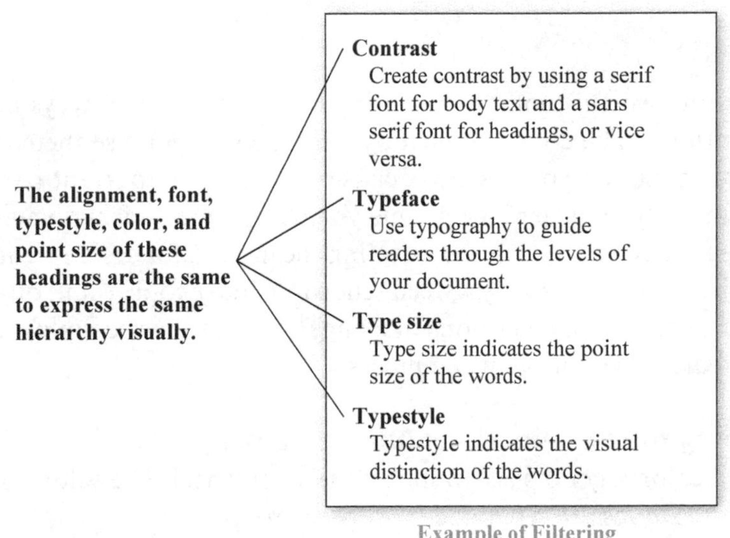

The alignment, font, typestyle, color, and point size of these headings are the same to express the same hierarchy visually.
Contrast
Create contrast by using a serif font for body text and a sans serif font for headings, or vice versa.
Typeface
Use typography to guide readers through the levels of your document.
Type size
Type size indicates the point size of the words.
Typestyle
Typestyle indicates the visual distinction of the words.

Example of Filtering

Filtering Patterns

Once you decide what the headings and subheadings should look like, be consistent with the design elements throughout the entire document.

Repetition

Repetition is an important design basic because it helps strengthen the overall look of the design. It also ties together different elements to help them remain organized and more consistent.

Grouping

Grouping is a tool for structuring document elements: text, pictures, icons, rules, bullets, and so on. By structuring these parts into visual units, grouping creates visual cohesion. Where figure–ground pulls images from a field, grouping organizes them into units and sub-units.

Grouping principles of visual elements:

- **Likeness in form** – Screen and table cell size, headings, typography, color
- **Spatial nearness** – Headings near the text, hypertext links
- **Division** – Title and navigational bars, frames, rules

By repeating and spatially arranging these elements, you construct visual patterns throughout the document that create cohesive groups.

COLOR

Color can be a powerful tool for presenting information. It conveys meaning and influences attitudes. The colors you choose and the way you use them together can have a strong impact on your users. Because color is an important part of design, you should carefully consider it each time you design a technical document.

Colors are largely responsible for dictating the mood of a design—each color has something a little different to say. Green tends to make people think of the environment or nature; red causes emotions like anger; blue is more calming and passive; and yellow creates a sensation of happiness.

Understanding the Relationships Among Colors

To understand color, a good place to start is the color wheel. The color wheel contains 12 hues. These 12 hues are separated into three groups:

- **Primary colors: red, blue, and yellow** – All other colors can be derived from these three.
- **Secondary colors: green, violet, and orange** – These colors are created by combining the primary colors.
- **Tertiary colors: red-orange, red-violet, blue-violet, blue-green, yellow-orange, and yellow-green** – These colors are made from combinations of the primary and secondary colors.

Color Wheel

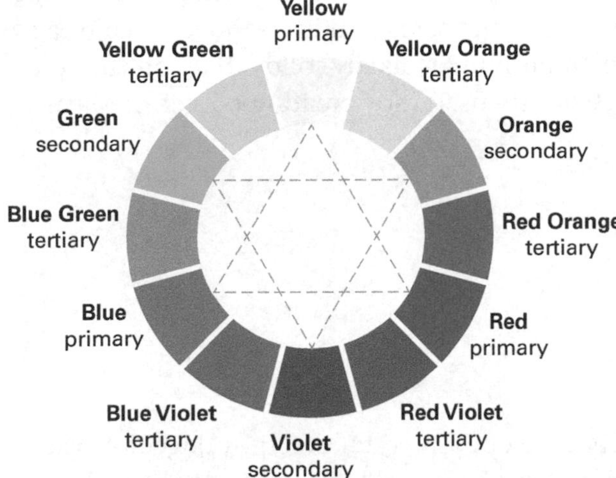

Colors have specific relationships, depending on their location on the color wheel.

- **Complementary colors** – Colors opposite each another on the color wheel. These colors contrast each other to create a dynamic effect.
- **Analogous colors** – Colors directly next to each other on the color wheel. Each color has two analogous colors (one on either side of it). Analogous colors used together create a harmonious and unified feeling because two of the colors contain the third.

Color Palette

One of the first steps in designing a text is to define a color palette that that you will adhere to. Following are five color schemes that you can define using the color wheel.

Monochromatic

Monochromatic color schemes are the simplest and are great for when you have a particular color in mind for creating a certain tone. To create a monochromatic color scheme, simply select one hue from the color wheel and pair it with various tones, shades, and tints of that hue.

Analogous

Analogous color schemes follow in simplicity, as they involve selecting neighboring hues on the color wheel. You might, for example, select blue as the focal color and then add blue-green and green, which both immediately follow blue on the color wheel. Analogous palettes are particularly useful for creating cooler or warmer moods in your documents.

Complementary

Complementary colors are colors that are opposite each other on the color wheel. Imagine the color wheel as a clock. A complement absorbs all the light waves the other color reflects and thus is the strongest contrast to the color.

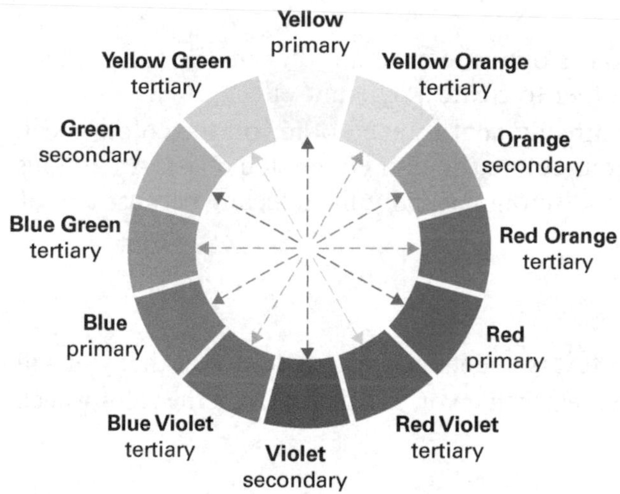

Complementary color schemes are easy to create: simply select two hues that are opposite each other on the color wheel, such as violet and yellow, or red and green. These color schemes can make a design especially attention grabbing. As is the case with analogous color schemes, the key to a color palette that works is to include a variety of tints and shades to give the palette variety that you can work with, with some lighter hues for a background, and some darker hues for text.

Split complementary

Split complementary color schemes are similar to traditional complementary schemes—the major difference being that instead of selecting the hue directly opposite of a hue, you will pick the two neighboring hues of that opposite hue. This is similar to a "peace sign" on the color wheel, giving you three colors to work with in your color scheme. For instance, instead of pairing yellow with purple, you could pair yellow with red-purple and blue-purple.

Triadic

Triadic color schemes involve selecting three hues that are equidistant along the color wheel. One of the most popular triadic color schemes, for example, is red, yellow, and blue. As always, it's good practice to select tints and shades of the hues you choose, so you end up with a subtle color palette.

Color Selection Tips

When you're choosing your colors, consider your audience. The challenge is to strike a balance between professionalism and attractiveness. The following tips may help you choose the appropriate colors for your audience.

Color combinations

Color combinations look different in online and paper formats. Test your document to verify that the colors work well together. Certain color combinations of text color on background color provide high contrast for ease of reading: white on black, green on purple, blue-green on red, and violet on yellow.

Visual filtering with color

Consistency and repetition is especially important when you select colors for documents because your readers will unconsciously look for patterns in all of the design elements in your technical publications: typefaces, alignment, type sizes, type styles, and especially color.

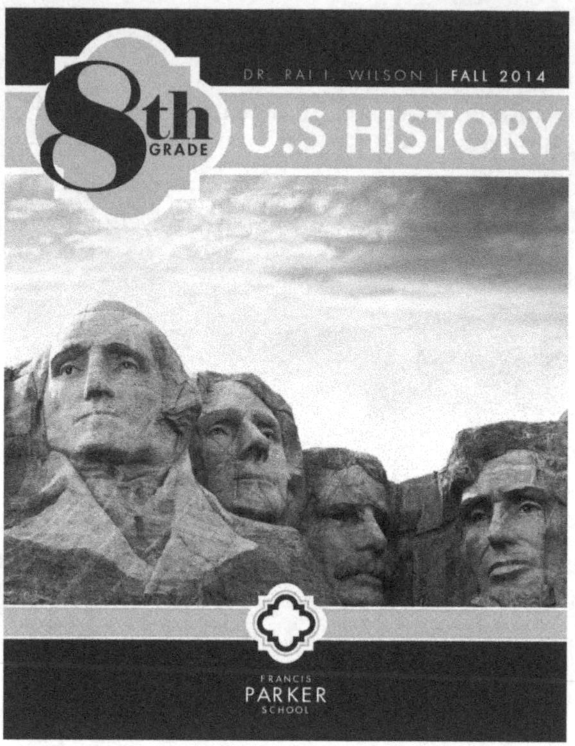

Sampling colors

You should draw colors from the images you use in the document. When using graphics in your documents, try to choose one or more colors from the graphic to use as text colors. The color combinations will tie the elements together for a uniform look.

Background colors

As a guideline, pick a background color and use two additional colors of text for maximum impact. Consider both color and texture for backgrounds. Sometimes a neutral background with a pleasing texture will work better than a solid color.

When using multiple background colors, consider using analogous colors; the colors will blend together without detracting from the foreground text. You can further contrast the foreground text by using a complementary text color.

Color purpose

Use colors sparingly for more effect and to avoid overwhelming the audience. Similar colors may interact differently; a slight variation can change the tone or feel of the information. Use color to indicate relationships between information, to convey a particular message, or to emphasize the information. If a particular color doesn't more clearly communicate the message, don't use that color.

Colors associations

The same information written in different colors can convey different meanings. For example, you can greatly emphasize the meaning of the word "Hot" by using red and orange font colors. A blue font, on the other hand, will detract from the meaning of the word. That being said there are some general rules about certain colors. Researchers, for example, have found that when humans view the color pink, it slows hormone production and creates a calming effect on the muscles. Other studies have found that people want to spend more time in rooms with blue or teal walls.

Below are common color associations and how you can use them to communicate a particular message.

COLOR	ASSOCIATIONS
Blue	Trustworthy, secure, and strong. Considered the safest color choice around the world, since it has many positive associations. Blue is one of the most common colors in signage and professional design because it has steadiness and power, but it's more friendly and approachable than black or gray.
Orange	Bold, creative, and playful. Orange can be a dangerous color because it's also one of the major colors that inspires the most aversion.
Purple	Royal, mysterious, and imaginative. Purple has long been associated with the social elite. It may also have childish associations, however.
Red	Exciting, aggressive, and important. Red often calls out for attention. Red is believed to be the first color that most cultures created a word for and thereby has one of the most primal and instinctive reactions.
Yellow	Energetic, youthful, and optimistic. Yellow is most often associated with light and the sun, so it is often used to show happiness and excitement.

Color in international documents

Certain colors have common associations in society, such as red with warning or green with go. Color associations can differ, however, depending on the nationality of your audience. It is difficult to generalize about color because the interpretation of color can change depending on the object displayed or how colors are combined. For example, a white lily and a white carnation represent mourning in France and Japan. The color white may not have a cultural meaning until it is combined with a flower. Similarly a color used in combination with other colors may carry a specific meaning. Red, white, and blue represent patriotism in the United States. However, red, white, and blue do not have a cultural meaning when they are used separately.

COLOR	INTERNATIONAL ASSOCIATIONS
Blue	**Western Cultures** – Represents trust, security, authority, loyalty, conservatism, business, peace, calm, serenity, depression, sadness, and masculinity. **Eastern Cultures** – Symbolizes immortality, wealth, and femininity. **Hinduism**– Strongly associated with Krishna, who embodies love and divine joy.
Red	**Western Cultures** – Symbolizes excitement, energy, passion, action, love, adventure, action, and danger. **Asian Cultures** – Symbolizes good luck, joy, prosperity, celebration, happiness, and a long life.
Orange	**Western Cultures** – Represents autumn, harvest, warmth, visibility, energy, vitality, excitement, adventure, creativity, caution, construction, harvest, and affordability. **Eastern Cultures** – Symbolizes love, happiness, humility, good health, and immortality. **Columbia** – Represents sexuality and fertility. **Hinduism** – Considered auspicious and sacred.
Green	**Western Cultures** – Represents luck, nature, freshness, spring, environmental awareness, wealth, inexperience, and jealousy. **Eastern Cultures** – Symbolizes youth, fertility, new life, eternity, regeneration, family, prosperity, and peace.
Yellow	**Western Cultures** – Associated with happiness, cheeriness, optimism, warmth, joy and hope, caution, cowardice, creativity, energy, awareness, hazards, warning, weakness, femininity. **Eastern Cultures** – Symbolizes love, happiness, humility, good health, sacredness, sovereignty, earth, power, royalty, and masculinity. **Egypt** – Conveys happiness and good fortune, prosperity, and mourning. **Germany** – Represents envy. **China** – Symbolizes sacredness, sovereignty, nourishment, royalty, honor, and masculinity. **Japan** – Represents courage, nobility, beauty, refinement, aristocracy, and cheerfulness. **Australia** – Associated with resurrection and rebirth.
White	**Western Cultures** – Symbolizes purity, elegance, peace, cleanliness, and virginity. Traditionally worn at weddings. **China, Korea, and Some Other Asian Countries** – Represents death, mourning, and bad luck. Traditionally worn at funerals. **Peru** – Associated with angels, good health, and time. **Hinduism** – Considered auspicious and sacred.

Common Color Modes

Different media of documents have different color modes. Computer screens display colors using RGB color values; browsers support hexadecimal color values; and color printers most often use CMYK color values.

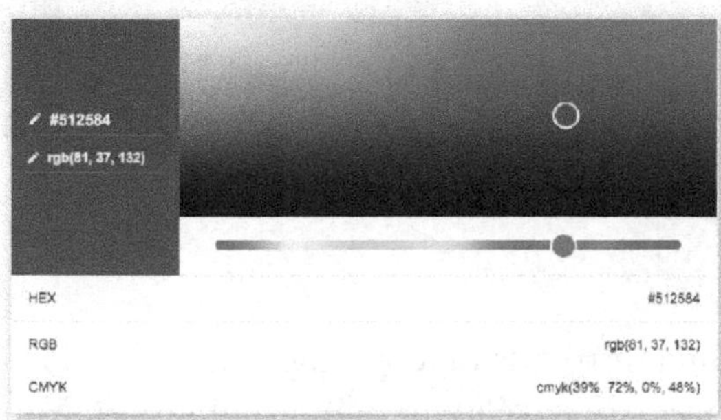

Hexadecimal colors

In HTML, colors are expressed as hexadecimal values. Hexadecimal color values are supported in all browsers. A hexadecimal color is specified with RR (red), GG (green) and BB (blue): #RRGGBB.

Hexadecimal integers between 00 and FF specify the intensity of the color. For example, #FF0000 is displayed as red, because red (RR) is set at its highest value (FF) and the others are set at 00.

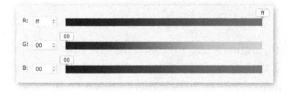

CMYK

This is one of the standard commercial printing color models. The initials stand for the semi-transparent "process" ink colors cyan (a kind of blue), magenta (the closest to red in process colors), yellow, and a key color, which is typically black. Tiny dots of the colors overlap one another, creating thousands of different colors with just four inks. When you print in full color on a commercial printing press using CYMK, it's referred to "four-color process."

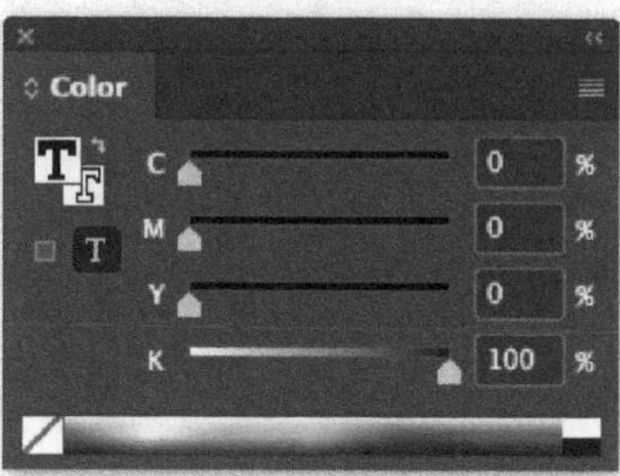

RGB

Color mode used for web and presentational purposes on computer monitors. This mode uses light to create colors. RGB images can have up to millions of colors. You should use the RGB mode for web pages, slides, computer presentations, and video, but never for images in documents that will be printed on a commercial printing press.

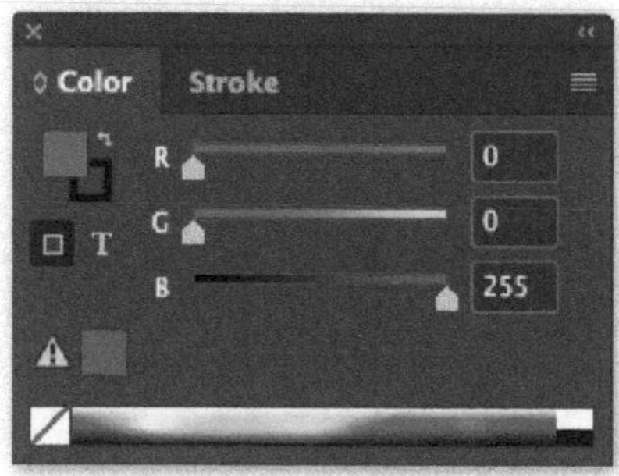

Each parameter (red, green, and blue) defines the intensity of the color as an integer between 0 and 255. For example, RGB (0, 0, 255) is rendered as blue, because the blue parameter is set to its highest value (255) and the others are set to 0.

Color and accessibility

According to different sources, five to eight percent of men have some form of color blindness, with red-green being the most common. For this reason, limit using red and green to high-contrast color combinations, and avoid relying entirely on color to present information.

ALIGNMENT

Alignment means, literally, how things line up. A composition that uses alignment to best effect controls how the readers' eyes move across a text. For instance, simply by having ragged-right margins and left alignment, you can increase reader comprehension of your technical documents by 10 percent.

- **Centered alignment** – A centered alignment causes the readers' eyes to move around the space with less determination, as they move from the end of one line and search for the beginning of the next.
- **Left alignment** – A strong left alignment gives the reader something to follow visually. Even elements that contrast in size, such as headings and subheadings, can demonstrate coherence through a single alignment.
- **Full justification** – Particularly with a monospaced typeface like Courier, fully justified text can lead to rivers of white. These are large white gaps created by a word-processing program attempting to align text on both the right and left margins.

Alignment and readability

Whether a text is left aligned, right aligned, or center aligned greatly affects its readability. Left alignment works best because it mirrors the way we read—from left to right. We know where each line ends and where the next begins.

ALIGNMENT

Left-aligned text	**Right-aligned text**
Center-aligned text and right-aligned text are generally harder to read, because your readers' eyes are used to following text from left to right.	Right-align your text if it against a left-aligned element, such as a margin, or left-aligned text block.
Center-aligned text	**Fully justified text**
Alignment is an important consideration in typography. How you choose to align your text can affect both your design goals and the readability of the text.	Particularly with a monospaced typeface such as Courier, fully justified text can lead to rivers of white. These are large white gaps created by a word-processing program attempting to align text on both the right and left margins.

HEADINGS

Readers of both text and visuals look for cues about what's important and how various elements are related to one another. Effective document design provides such cues through headings and subheadings. Clear headings and subheadings help your readers navigate by showing the document's hierarchy of ideas. Appropriately aligned headings guide the reader's eye across a page, screen, or interface.

Creating Access Aids for Technical Content: Headings

Good headings help readers in a number of ways. The purpose of a heading is to help communicate the content that is under it. Well-written headings in well-organized text help readers by doing the following:

- Providing readers with a quick overview (advance organizer) of what is on the page.
- Setting the context for each section.
- Facilitating scanning, so readers can find the information they need.
- Creating focal points, which makes technical information less dense and more readable.

Organization

Simply labeling headings is not sufficient for readers who skim and scan information. Organize your headings in a recognizable way—chronologically or alphabetically—so readers can skim and scan the document to quickly find the information they need.

An easy way to organize your information is by outlining the document by its headings and subheadings, similar to a two-level table of contents.

1982–1984: Laying the Foundation	**15**
The Early Years	17
Creating Adobe Systems	23
Steve Jobs and the LaserWriter	33

Heading Styles

The headings in your document should be brief, clear, informative, and five or fewer words. Effective professional writers maintain parallel phrasing and consistent capitalization, regardless of the typeface or style they choose. Once you decide what the headings and subheadings should look like, be consistent with comparable headings and subheadings throughout the entire document.

HEADING STYLE	TECHNICAL COMMUNICATIONS BEST USED WITH	EXAMPLES
Imperative mood verb phrases and -ing (gerund) phrases	Action-oriented labels common in instructional materials.	Start your free trial Adjusting the scale of your shapes Tell powerful stories Using the typesetting features

(continued)

HEADING STYLE	TECHNICAL COMMUNICATIONS BEST USED WITH	EXAMPLES
Noun phrases	Labels common to technical descriptions and informational documents.	Analytics that everyone loves A Breakout for Data Integration Powerful 3D Data Visualization
Questions	Common with medical writing and types of documents readers typically go to with questions, such as policy and procedures, employee handbooks, and FAQs.	How Can I Manage My Diabetes? How does what you eat affect diabetes? Can I Treat Diabetes Without Drugs?

Heading Levels

The relative size and prominence of the section headings in a document indicate how it is structured and which sections are most important. Headings also name the sections so that readers know where they are and where they are going. Headings focus the attention of readers while providing a useful pathway through complex technical documents, such as lab reports, proposals, and computer documentation. The style of the headings offers readers visuals cues for content, navigation, and organization. Clearly differentiating the headings from body-text in your design makes your technical documents easier to read and use and creates the difference between whether your readers will have to scrutinize every word or be able to skim and scan for key points.

Use typographical conventions to distinguish between body-text and headings as well as the different levels of elements (heading 1, heading 2, captions) within your document. Once you determine what a first-level heading should look like—Calibri or Gill Sans, for example—always be consistent with comparable headings throughout your document. For short documents with short sections, use a design of a page title and one level of headings. For longer documents, use a design of a page title and two levels of headings.

Capitalization

You have two options for capitalizing words in titles, headings, subheadings, and captions. Whichever style you choose, be consistent.

- **Sentence capitalization** – Capitalize the first word of the heading and nothing else except for proper nouns.
- **Traditional Title Capitalization** – Capitalize all words except for articles (a, an, the), conjunctions (and, or, but), and prepositions with fewer than five letters (to, at)—unless one of these words begins the heading.

Typography in Headings

Another method to aid your readers' understanding is in choosing the most appropriate font. Use a legible sans serif typeface for titles, headings, and subheadings.

Alignment of Headings

In addition to being consistent in the typography and phrasing of your headings, you should consistently place and align your headings along the same vertical line.

TYPES OF HEADINGS	EXAMPLES
Modified left-hanging indented headings	**Bold 12 pt. Sans Serif Heading 1** In presentational writing, you should try to minimize elaboration. One effective method by using bulleted lists. When using lists, you should have no more than seven elements.
Sidebar headings	**Bold 12 pt. Sans Serif Heading 1** In presentational writing, you should try to minimize elaboration. One effective method by using bulleted lists. When using lists, you should have no more than seven elements.
Run-in headings	**Bold 12 pt. Sans Serif Heading 1** The following run-in headings allow your readers to understand information at a glance: • **Paragraphs** – Your paragraphs should have no more than 35 words and no more than 3 sentences. • **Visual Elements** – Paper documentation typically employs listings, headings, subheadings, sectional overviews, textual introductions, and captioning for visual elements.

Punctuation in Headings

A form of punctuation such as a colon is not necessary with modified left-hanging indented headings and with sidebar headings. Run-in headings, however, can take a variety of forms of punctuation: an en dash, a colon, a period, or a hyphen.

LISTS

With the exception of your resume, look for every opportunity to use a vertical list in your professional writing documents.

Introductions to Lists – Advance Organizers

To provide a context (schema) for your readers, introduce with a narrative each section, each visual, and each list in professional writing documents. Your readers should already understand the purpose of each of these before they read them.

Number of Items in Lists

When using lists in paper documents, you should have no more than seven elements. With electronic documents, you should have no more than five. Avoid one-item lists of any type.

TYPE OF LIST	TECHNICAL COMMUNICATIONS BEST USED WITH
Numerical	Common with instructional materials or materials that follow sequence or order.
Bulleted	Used with lists with no sequence or order.
Alphabetical	Like numerical lists, alphabetical lists have sequence or order. To avoid confusion, use alphabetical lists only when instructed to in a house style guide.
Run-in headings	Run-in headings function as scannable advance organizers by providing a topic word or phrase for each sentence or paragraph they run into.

Capitalization and Punctuation

Always capitalize the first word of a list item. Similar to a sentence, never begin a list item with a numeral.

- **Introductions to lists** – Never follow verbs with colons in the introduction of a list. Rather, use a complete-sentence introduction.
- **Terminal punctuation of lists** – Use terminal punctuation (periods) with verb phrases or complete sentences. For all other types of lists, such as single words and noun phrases, use no punctuation.

Alignment

Indent all lists and set the tabs to bring the text close to the bullets or numbers.

Incorrect

The following fonts are suitable for body text:

- Cambria
- Garamond

Correct

The following fonts are suitable for headings, subheadings, and small point sizes:

- Helvetica
- Calibri

Bullets in Lists

Use standard bullets in lists.

Incorrect

The following fonts are suitable for body text:

➢ Cambria
➢ Garamond

Correct

The following fonts are suitable for headings, subheadings, and small point sizes:

- Helvetica
- Calibri

Paragraph Spacing

Increase the paragraph spacing in longer lists, particularly those with run-in headings, to increase readability.

Incorrect

The following run-in headings allow your readers to assimilate information at a glance:

- **Paragraphs** – Your paragraphs should have no more than 35 words and no more than 3 sentences. Bolding key words, phrases, or sentences allows you to provide additional schemata by providing your reader with a visual overview.
- **Sentences** – Your sentences should have no more than 17 words.
- **Visual Elements** – Paper documentation typically employs lists, headings, subheadings, sectional overviews, textual introductions, and captions for visual elements. Additional elements such as ragged-right margins can increase your readers' comprehension by 10 percent.

Correct

The following run-in headings allow your readers to assimilate information at a glance:

- **Paragraphs** – Your paragraphs should have no more than 35 words and no more than three sentences. Bolding key words, phrases, or sentences allows you to provide additional schemata by providing your reader with a visual overview.

- **Sentences** – Your sentences should have no more than 17 words.

- **Visual Elements** – Paper documentation typically employs listings, headings, subheadings, sectional overviews, and textual introductions and captioning for visual elements. Additional elements such as ragged-right margins can increase your readers' comprehension by 10 percent.

DISCUSSION 3.1

Critique the following list for problems with the introduction, typography, punctuation, type of list, spacing, alignment, and capitalization. How would you revise it?

I have gathered data on different health insurance plans and companies and compared them using six criteria to make my recommendation. My criteria are:

1. availability in Alaska,
2. premiums,
3. annual deductible,
4. out-of-pocket limit,
5. emergency room, and
6. hospitalization.

VISUAL DESIGN LEARNING THEORIES

Three principles, based on research into how people learn, can help you to design effective texts.

Chunking

Chunking, or clustering, is the function of grouping together information related by perceptual features. This is a form of semantic relation (any relationship between two or more words based on their meanings), such as brands of laptops, items in a list, or MLB teams. Readers understand and retain technical information best if you deliver it with an obvious semantic relation.

DISCUSSION 3.2

What is the semantic relationship of the items in this bulleted list?

- Visual Elements
- Computer documentation should have the following visual elements:
- Sectional overviews (advance organizers)
- Numerical lists
- Headings
- Screenshots
- Callouts

Chunking limits

Research indicates that the average person can process and remember a limited amount of information based upon the media and complexity of the information. These limits are expressed as channel capacity.

Channel Capacity

The amount of space the human brain has for certain kinds of information. Chunking allows the brain to increase the channel capacity of the short-term memory; however, each chunk must be meaningful to the individual.

Schema Theory

To organize a document, particularly one with technical information, you must proceed in an informed and systematic way, considering the readers and purpose to be more effective. Cognitive psychologists have found that the most accepted theory of learning is the schema theory. According to this theory, readers base their interpretation of texts on prior knowledge and expectations of the subject matter.

- People store information in long-term memory by creating schemata—conceptual frameworks—for facts and concepts.
- Each stored schema becomes a pattern or template against which new information can be matched.
- This stored schema can then be used to process new information.

This theory explains why analogy is such a useful teaching tool. Analogies relate new information to familiar information. It also explains why learners with expertise on a subject can learn new material on the subject more quickly than can equally intelligent learners with limited knowledge on the subject.

LAYOUT GRIDS & TYPOGRAPHY MATRICES

Layout Grids

A grid divides a page or screen into a series of squares upon which you can organize content: text or graphics. Grids are used in the layout of almost all professional magazines, books, newspapers, and websites to group and organize information consistently. Visual consistency increases user comfort and security as well as reduces the time required to locate and process information. Grids ensure consistency in the type, order, appearance, and placement of information on a page or interface.

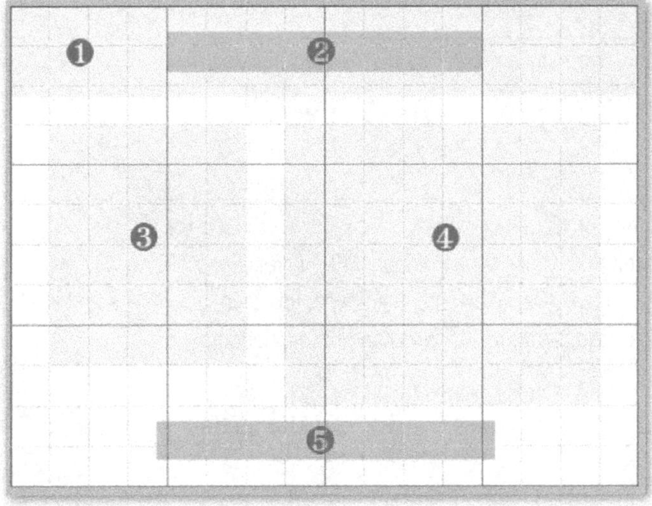

Layout Grid

Typography Matrices

Accessibility, consistency, and predictability are essential characteristics for a well-designed technical document, be it a paper publication or an online help system. The most efficient and consistent way to lay out a technical document is by constructing a layout grid and a typography matrix that supports it.

Techniques for maintaining consistency and regularity include the following:

- Using a standard color scheme
- Using a consistent layout
- Repeating the typeface, type size, and typestyle for particular elements
- Repeating the size and spacing of elements

A typography matrix may include much more detail, but the elements identified in a typical matrix include the following.

CLASSIFICATION	ELEMENT
Document Layout	Page/screen size (pixels, picas, inches, percentage)
	Page orientation (portrait, landscape, custom)
	Margins, gutters, binding width
	Color model (CMYK, RGB, Pantone, Hexadecimal)
	Tables (borders, padding, size in pixels or percentages)
	Navigation bars (color, placement, graphic format)
	Captions (format, placement, size, color)

CLASSIFICATION	ELEMENT
Typography	Typefaces Type styles Point sizes Colors
Visuals and Graphics	Graphic format (PNG, JPEG, TIFF) Graphic resolution (DPI – Dots Per Inch, PPI – Pixels Per Inch) Rules (length, thickness, color, compound type, join type, arrow type and size) Callout types (tag, sentence, legends and notes, headings)

For example, this typography matrix corresponds with the earlier layout grid.

TYPOGRAPHY MATRIX

Canvas	**Size** 550 px x 400 px	**Color** R=255 G=102 B=51			
Module 1	**Color** R=103 G=70 B=167	**Fill** 100%	**Opacity** 100%		
Module 2	**Text** Callibri Bold 12 pt.	**Color** R=255 G=255 B=255	**Alignment** centered	**Rule** R=255 G=255 B=255 Length: 1p7 Thickness: 1pt.	**Case** Trad. title cap.
Module 3	**Width x Height** 13p7.49 x 6p3.021	**Graphic Format** tiff	**Resolution** 72 ppi		
Module 4	**Title** Callibri Bold 10 pt. Trad. title cap. **Body** Callibri 9 pt.	**Color** R=0 G=0 B=0	**Alignment** left	**Case** Trad. title cap.	
Module 5	**Hyperlink line** Callibri 9 pt. **Copyright line** Callibri 8 pt.	**Link Text Color** R=103 G=70 B=167 **Color** R=0 G=0 B=0	**Pipe Color** R=0 G=0 B=0 **Alignment** centered	**Alignment** centered	**Case** lowercase

Another benefit to using a grid structure is that you can move elements from page to page, and the movement will not seem random; rather it will show a repeated underlying visual system. By referencing the grid and moving elements by proportional and consistent increments, you establish a unifying and discernible pattern. Then as users grow familiar with the page design, they can read, scan, or skim each individual page much more efficiently and effectively.

DISCUSSION 3.3

With the same horizontal and vertical orientation, this grid does not encourage reading in a specific sequence. How might the author redesign the grid to force the reader to read in a particular order?

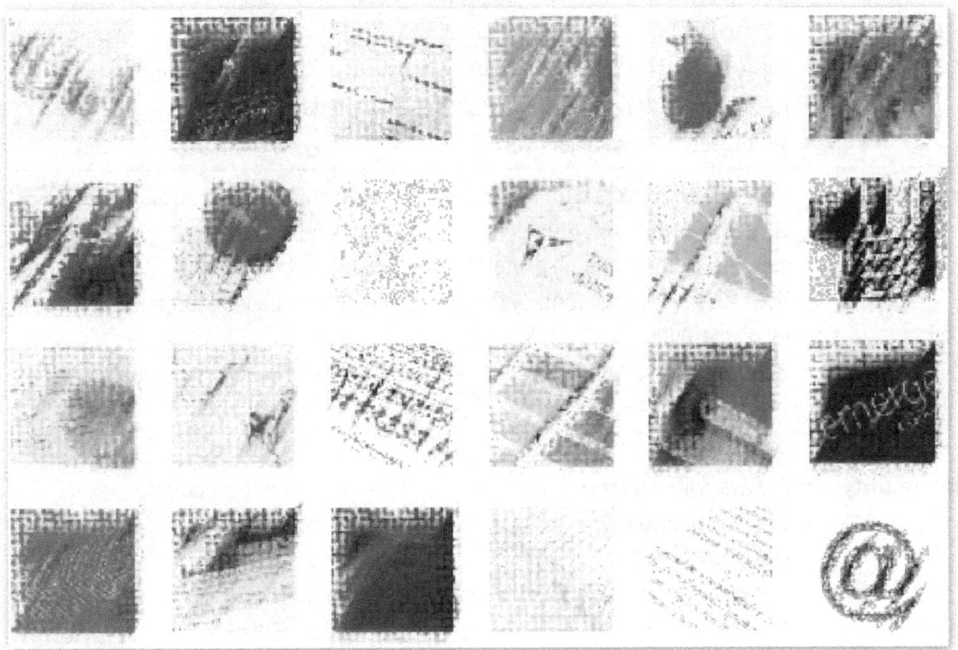

VISUAL DESIGN QUICK REFERENCE

Design	• Follow the client's style guide or create a new one with your client. • Design for the audience's tastes. • Use a grid as a guide for arranging the document's elements. • Use a limited color palette of harmonious colors. • Use the same color for each category. • Limit the number of typefaces to two, a sans serif and a serif typeface. • Use metaphors and themes consistently. • Place navigational elements and access aids the same place on every page or screen. • Usability test the document.
Style	• Use words and phrases common to the reader. • Have only one idea per paragraph. • Write concisely (generally half the word count of conventional writing). • Have a line length of 80 characters or 10-12 words per line. • Write factually and objectively.
Legibility	• **Colors** – Use colors with high contrast between the text and background. • **Backgrounds** – Use either plain color backgrounds or backgrounds with extremely subtle patterns. Patterns disrupt the readers to recognize words. • **Font Size** – Use tiny fonts (<11 point) in footnotes, headers, footers, captions, and legal disclaimers. • **Fonts** – Use typography appropriately. Research has shown that sans serif fonts are easier to read on monitors and that serif fonts are easier to read in dense blocks of text.
Scannability	• Always, with no exceptions, design the document with focal points. • Include an advance organizer at the beginning of each section and a summary at the end of each section. • Use black characters against a white background for maximum figure–ground contrast. • Avoid fully justified text, except for small word blocks or single words. • Use ragged-right alignment to increase readability. • Use both upper- and lowercase characters, rather than all uppercase words. • Limit underlining to hyperlinks. • Design with visual queuing and filtering in mind: body text size: 11–12 point minimum, heading 1 size: 12–14 point maximum. • Design with abundant white space. • Use an outline to create meaningful headings and subheadings. • Use vertical lists (numerical, bulleted, and run-in headings) whenever possible.

EXERCISE 3.1 – PAGE DESIGN

Using the principles of visual design discussed in the chapter, write a memorandum critiquing the following document for readability, then discuss how you would redesign it.

MEMORANDUM

McNeil Informatics
1122 KING AVE
Kingsville, TX USA

TO: Denise McNeil

From: Rochelle Sweet, Assistant to the CEO

Subject: Corporate Proposal Inquiries

Date: January 27, 2027

Purpose: The purpose of this memo is to point out the personal and ethical ramifications that could occur should you choose to omit, disguise and or delete important facts that would be personally biased toward employees, management the company, and jeopardize the contract itself.

Summary: Allowing personal biases and or preconceived opinions by way of another's body language could be misinterpreted and thus cause irreparable harm to employees jeopardizing internal stability by way of emotional and financial stability and also by them feeling that in order for you to obtain a contract you would invalidate their position as well as giving them their just due Without more information from your staff as well as how Crescent Petroleum founders truly feel concerning your reservations, I don't see that a professional decision whether to accept or bypass this contract can be formed.

Discussion: It is my understanding, from overhearing your conversation with Mr. Lipton, that you are considering omitting names not giving credit where it's due from the boilerplate when this proposal is drafted. My concern is that you would not only be selling yourself short but the company. As it is, this policy is not based on whether a person may like you for your gender or ethnicity but whether or not you can and will do the job professionally, accurately, and expeditiously.

Conclusion: It is therefore with great respect I suggest there be an all-staff meeting to discuss the pros and cons of this decision, get more ideas and weigh whether or not our company would benefit from this transaction or if it would be worth all the potential chaos it could cause. Thank you for your time & consideration in this matter.

Credits

Fig. 3.4a: Copyright © 2017 Depositphotos/photokirov@mail.ru.

Fig. 3.4b: Copyright © 2016 Depositphotos/leungchopan.

Fig. 3.4d: Copyright © 2013 Depositphotos/3dmentat.

Fig. 3.12: Copyright © 2011 Depositphotos/kamchatka.

Fig. 3.13: Copyright © by Adobe Systems Incorporated.

Fig. 3.14: Copyright © by Adobe Systems Incorporated.

Fig. 3.15: Copyright © by Adobe Systems Incorporated.

Fig. 3.16: Copyright © by Adobe Systems Incorporated.

CHAPTER FOUR

Cognitive Theories in Professional Writing

SCHEMA THEORY

Schema theory has become a widely accepted theory of human cognition. According to cognitive scientists, users know what to do when they encounter a particular type of problem based on previous experience. They store information in long-term memory by creating knowledge structures called "schemata" for concepts and facts and to understand and remember them. Each stored schema then becomes a pattern or template against which new information can be matched. According to schema theory, meaningful learning occurs when an individual can tie new information to concepts within his or her schema. Similarly, the most effectively designed technical writing documents are those that provide for a mental scaffold, context, or schema into which new information can be plugged.

Cognitive Scaffolding

Information in long-term memory is that which has been learned and can be retrieved on demand. One of the goals of effective technical writing, particularly with instructional materials, is to create instruction that assists learners in making information enter and be retained in long-term memory. When we use stored schema to process new information, we can modify the existing schema and make it more complex, or we may create a new schema.

For example, the typical outline most high school students in the United States have to create for their high school research papers is analogous to designing a page or interface using the new concept of visual queuing. It also explains why learners with expertise on a subject can learn new material on the subject more quickly than can equally intelligent learners with limited knowledge on the subject.

Using Schema Theory to Present Technical Information

Readers actively interpret documents as they work with them. They base their interpretation on a number of aspects:

- Prior knowledge, experience, and expectations they have about the subject matter
- Type of document
- Structure of the document
- Context in which they are reading the document

Creating or Modifying Schema

As new information is stored in previously formed schema, the schema is continuously restructuring and redeveloping, changing how learners see and interpret the world.

Perceived Structure

Users seek and use visual structure to scan and skim information quickly for relevant information. Users perceive what they expect, and their expectations are formed by three factors:

- Their past experiences
- The current context
- Their goals and plans for the future

An example of perceived structure is a five-paragraph essay. Readers experienced with a five-paragraph essay would expect to see an introduction that outlines the essay in the first paragraph, three supporting paragraphs, and a conclusion that summarizes the essay. Successful documents are those that make explicit connections to readers' prior knowledge and expectations.

Methods to achieve schema in technical communication include the following:

- Introductions, overviews, and summaries to entire documents, sections, and chapters (advance organizers)
- Descriptive or action-oriented titles, headings, subheadings, and run-in headings
- Textual references to lists and visuals
- Textual references that appear before and on the same page as visuals
- Useful captions for visuals and illustrations: descriptive labels
- Periodic sentences with new, difficult, and important information appearing near the ends of the sentences
- Consistent placement of information and use of typography

Moreover, these factors should guide your decisions when you design a technical document:

- Avoid ambiguity. Everyone should interpret your design the same way.
- Be consistent.
- Understand the user's goals.

Top-Down Processing

These factors should also determine how you structure your technical writing. For most types of technical writing documents, you should arrange the major points first. The majority of learners move from general to specific or from the concept to details.

Similarly, the document should have design elements that allow for creating schemata:

- Headings
- Overviews
- Parallelism in headings, lists, titles, chapters
- Introduction to lists
- Typographical conventions like different typefaces, point sizes, and type styles

Schema Structures

Successful technical documents are those that make explicit connections to readers' prior knowledge and expectations. Readers form schema structures by their experiences with a particular type or genre of writing, including:

- Correspondence
- Instructions
- Proposals
- Technical descriptions

Principles of Organizing Technical Information to Facilitate Learning

When writing for organization, follow these principles:

TABLE 4.1

METHOD TO CREATE OR MODIFY EXISTING SCHEMA	CHARACTERISTICS
Follow pre-established document structures.	Technical writers and editors should ensure that the structure of a document conforms to a prescribed structure.
Arrange information from general to specific.	Conceptual information that orients readers belongs at the beginning of textual documents. Moreover, while beginners need more explanation than experts, all readers learn new information more easily if it is preceded by familiar information.
Apply conventional patterns of organization.	These are familiar organizational patterns for presenting technical information: • **Chronological**: Narratives, instructions, process analysis • **Spatial**: Technical descriptions • **Comparison/contrast**: Feasibility studies • **Cause-effect**: Proposals
Group related material.	Chapters should not mix unrelated information, and lists should develop meaningfully rather than randomly.

TECHNICAL WRITING GENRES

The natural structuring of a text based upon its genre provides a mental scaffold. For example, in the procedural genre, the writer's intent is to provide instructions on how to do something. Much the same as advance organizers, the concept of semantic structures is widely accepted in discourse analysis and cognitive psychology as an organizational principle of texts for creating schema, and in turn, cognitive scaffolding.

Cognitive Scaffolding Using Document Structures

TABLE 4.2

DOCUMENT STRUCTURE	PURPOSE
Beginning	Presents the concept by identifying the topic and by placing it into a context: background, purpose, significance, middle, and end.
Middle	Analyzes the overall topic by identifying component parts and develops the topic with details.
End	Considers the topic as a whole by summarizing, drawing conclusions, or anticipating applications of the information.

DEPTH OF PROCESSING

Information that is analyzed deeply is better recalled than information that is analyzed superficially. Thinking about information improves the likelihood that the information will be recalled later.

This results from the two ways in which information is processed:

- **Maintenance rehearsal** – An example is repeating a phone number back to yourself. No additional analysis is performed on the information.
- **Elaborative rehearsal** – This type of rehearsal involves deeper, more intricate analysis of information. An example is reading a passage, then having to answer questions about the meaning of the passage. This typically results in two to three times better recall than maintenance rehearsal.

Determining factors of how deeply information is processed are the following:

- **Distinctiveness of information** – The degree to which the information is unique to the user's previous experience and the surrounding information.
- **Relevance of information** – The degree to which the user perceives the information to be important.
- **Degree of elaboration** – How much thought is required to interpret and understand the information.

Deep processing of information that involves these factors result in the best possible recall and retention of information. Deep processing requires more concentration and effort than mere exposure, such as the case of a classroom lecture, for example.

When to Consider Levels of Processing Approach

You should use depth of processing in designing technical documents where recall and retention of information is important.

- Use unique presentation and interesting activities to engage the reader to deeply process information.
- Use case studies, examples, and other textual devices to make information relevant to users.

PERFORMANCE LOAD

Performance load is the degree of mental and physical activity required to achieve a goal. The greater the effort to accomplish a task, the less likely the task will be accomplished successfully. If the performance load is high, performance time and errors increase and the probably of successfully accomplishing the goal decreases. If the performance load is low, performance time and errors decrease and the probability of successfully accomplishing the goal increases.

Performance load consists of two types:

- Cognitive load
- Kinematic load

Cognitive Load

The amount of mental activity—perception, memory, and rehearsal—required to accomplish a goal. An example of this is when the graphical user interface replaced the command line interface in computer operating systems, which dramatically reduced the mental effort required to memorize the commands necessary to use a computer.

FIGURE 4.1 Command Line Interface

```
Displays a list of files and subdirectories in a directory.

DIR [drive:][path][filename] [/P] [/W] [/A[[:]attribs]] [/O[[:]sortord]]
    [/S] [/B] [/L] [/C[H]]

  [drive:][path][filename]   Specifies drive, directory, and/or files to list.
  /P        Pauses after each screenful of information.
  /W        Uses wide list format.
  /A        Displays files with specified attributes.
  attribs    D  Directories    R  Read-only files         H  Hidden files
             S  System files   A  Files ready to archive  -  Prefix meaning "not"
  /O        List by files in sorted order.
  sortord    N  By name (alphabetic)       S  By size (smallest first)
             E  By extension (alphabetic)  D  By date & time (earliest first)
             G  Group directories first    -  Prefix to reverse order
             C  By compression ratio (smallest first)
  /S        Displays files in specified directory and all subdirectories.
  /B        Uses bare format (no heading information or summary).
  /L        Uses lowercase.
  /C[H]     Displays file compression ratio; /CH uses host allocation unit size.

Switches may be preset in the DIRCMD environment variable.  Override
preset switches by prefixing any switch with - (hyphen)--for example, /-W.

C:\>_
```

FIGURE 4.2

Strategies for Reducing Cognitive Load

You should design technical documents to minimize performance load to the greatest degree possible:

- Chunk information that users need to remember
- Reduce visual noise
- Provide memory aids to assist in complex tasks
- Automate memory-intensive tasks

CHANNEL CAPACITY

The amount of space in the human brain for certain kinds of information. This is the reason that the telephone number is seven digits. Bell wanted the number to be as long as possible. But time and time again, tests have shown this natural limit of intellectual capacity.

Examples

- No more than nine bullet points on a bulleted list
- No more than nine steps in a set of instructions
- No more than nine bullet points on a slide

Writers should classify the information into smaller logically related groups and introduce a subheading.

CHUNKING PRINCIPLE

The chunking principle suggests the number (channel capacity) that people could be reliably expected to keep in their short-term or working memory a few minutes after having been told these numbers only once. The chunking principle suggests that all texts should be divided into relatively small units of information of about the amount that humans can handle with their short-term memory limitations, typically five to nine elements. For online documents, this number is even smaller.

Chunking Limits

Chunking limits are the result of research that indicates the average person can process and remember an amount of information based on the media and complexity of the information.

Paper chunking limit

7 ± 2 pieces of simple information
5 ± 2 pieces of more complex information

Online chunking limit

5 ± 1 pieces of information

STRUCTURED WRITING

The main tenets of structuring technical writing:

TABLE 4.3

STRUCTURED WRITING CONCEPT	CHARACTERISTICS	APPLICATION FOR TECHNICAL COMMUNICATORS
Chunking	The chunking principle suggests that all of the text should be divided into relatively small units of information of about the amount that humans can handle with their short-term memory limitations.	Lists, paragraphs, or chapters and sections
Relevancy	Conceptual information that orients readers belongs at the beginning of textual documents. Moreover, while beginners need more explanation than experts, all readers learn new information more easily if it is preceded by familiar information.	Instructional materials, technical descriptions and technical definitions, and exemplification
Labeling	Labels every information chunk and block according to specific criteria: • **Clear** – Use labels that clearly describe the function or content of the block of information. • **Brief** – Make labels brief. Shorter labels are better than longer ones as long as they don't introduce ambiguity. In general use no more than 3–5 words. • **Consistent** – Use the same vocabulary in the label that you use in the block. • **Familiar** – Use vocabulary in the label that is generally familiar to target users.	Useful, descriptive titles, headings, subheadings

TABLE 4.3 (continued)

STRUCTURED WRITING CONCEPT	CHARACTERISTICS	APPLICATION FOR TECHNICAL COMMUNICATORS
Consistency	These are familiar organizational patterns for presenting technical information: • **Chronological** – Narratives, instructions, process analysis • **Spatial** – Technical descriptions • **Comparison/contrast** – Feasibility studies • **Cause–effect** – Proposals	Similar words, labels, format, organizations, and sequences for similar subject matter

SERIAL POSITIONING EFFECT

Serial positioning effect is the tendency for users to be far more likely to remember items presented at the beginning or at the end of a list than items in the middle. The tendency to remember an item in the first position within a sequence is the *primacy effect*, and the tendency to remember an item in last position is the *regency effect*.

Primacy Effect

The primacy effect occurs because the initial items in a list are stored in long-term memory more efficiently than items later in a list. In lists where items are rapidly presented, the primacy effect is weaker because users have less time to store the initial items in their long-term memories. For visual stimuli, items you present early in a list have the greatest influence. Not only are they better recalled, they also influence the user's interpretation of later items.

Regency Effect

The regency effect occurs because the last few items in a list are still in the user's working memory and readily available. For auditory stimuli, items you present late in a list have the greatest influence.

Order Effect

An order effect is when the first and last items in a list are more likely to be selected than items in the middle. An example of this effect is how the order of candidates on a ballot influences voters.

Application for Designing Technical Documents

Present important items at the beginning or end of a list to maximize recall.

- **Visual information** – When the list is visual you should present important information at the beginning.
- **Auditory information** – When the list is auditory you should present important information at the end. In decision-making situations, if a decision is to be made immediately after the presentation of the last item, you increase the probability of an item being selected by presenting it at the end.

ADVANCE ORGANIZERS

The advance organizer approach to teaching is a cognitive instructional strategy used to promote the learning and retention of new information. The concept of advance organizers has become among the most widely used methods of instruction in primary and secondary schools in the past 50 years.

This approach encourages students to build upon prior knowledge and mentally organize their thoughts before being introduced to new concepts. To enhance meaningful learning, students preview information to be learned. Teachers do this by providing a brief introduction about the way the information is structured. In presenting these outlines of information, teachers help students see the big picture to be learned. By making new material more familiar and meaningful to students, it becomes easier to retrieve.

This teaching strategy maintains that the most important object a child could bring to a learning situation is what he or she already knows. According to this approach meaningful learning results when that child ties new information to relevant concepts within his or her schema. Therefore, when the child is able to make this connection, a series of changes occurs within his or her entire cognitive structure. Pre-existing concepts are modified, and new associations between concepts are formed. Thus, the most important element of meaningful learning is not so much how information is presented but how new information is integrated into an existing knowledge base.

Although proposed almost 50 years ago, this cognitive strategy for organizing technical information continues to be relevant to technical communicators today. But this approach has been limited for the most part to the classroom and has not seen widespread discussion and application in scientific and technical communication theory and practice. Advance organizers have progressed far beyond being simply an effective teaching strategy for classroom instruction. By using these methods technical writers can create documents that allow readers to access and retain information easily.

Contemporary Cognitive Science Associations

The advance organizer approach to teaching builds upon schema theory in promoting the learning and retention of new information by linking it to past knowledge. According to this theory, meaningful learning occurs when an individual is able to tie new information to concepts within his or her schema. Advance organizers thus help users learn and retain technical information by providing a mental scaffold or schema into which they can plug new information.

APPLICATIONS FOR TECHNICAL WRITING

Advance organizers are particularly useful in the field of technical communication. Advance organizers use familiar terms and concepts to link what the reader already knows to the new information that will be presented in the material. This aids in the process of transforming knowledge and applying it to new situations, as well as embedding the new information into the user's long-term memory.

Particularly with technical material, the most effective document structure is one that uses connections with readers' prior knowledge to trigger appropriate schema. Readers actively interpret documents as they work through them, and the basis for this interpretation is their prior knowledge and the expectations they have about the subject matter, the type and structure of the document, and the semantic context in which they are reading the document.

In the absence of this knowledge, the advance organizer provides an effective cognitive scaffold: advance organizers have been found to be effective text adjuncts in compensating for the absence of relevant, existing schemata in the learner.

Research has shown that advance organizers do not have to be lengthy or complex to be effective; something as simple as a meaningful title may be useful in facilitating the learning process.

Categories of Advance Organizers

Advance organizers may take several different forms, but ultimately, they all serve the same purpose: to provide information—textual, graphical, or verbal—that announces the background, purpose, scope, or organization of the discussion that follows them, thereby previewing and providing a context for the information that follows. The following table categorizes advance organizers by their function as well as the medium in which they occur.

Contextual	Contextual advance organizers give a mental context for processing new material or provide a link to pre-existing schemata. These often are presented at a higher level of abstraction than the information they precede.
Overviews and previews	Previewing technical material is one of the most common and effective types of advance organizers.
Introductions	The advance organizer presented in the introduction of an oral presentation to prepare the audience for the main points that will be covered is arguably the most important element in an entire presentation.
Run-in headings	This type of heading provides schema by providing a context for the text in the sentence or paragraph it "runs into," much the same as a topic sentence in a paragraph.

Textual references to visuals	These works to preview the information and provide a mental context for the information.
Glossaries	This type of advance organizer uses familiar terms and concepts to link what the user already knows to unfamiliar terms.
Navigational	Used effectively, this type of advance organizers creates a mental map of a document, website, or menu—a mental scaffold that helps users find and process the information contained within.
Tables of content	Previewing technical material is one of the most common and effective types of advance organizers.
Titles, headings, and subheadings	Clear headings and subheadings help readers to process information by showing the document's hierarchy of ideas.
Menus and navigational bars	Menus and navigational bars give readers a sense of hierarchy and location similar to a table of contents.
Sitemaps	A sitemap is a visual representation of a website's structure, organization, flow, and grouping of content and information. Sitemaps are useful for websites with complex, multi-path structures. Sitemaps establish visual hierarchy, which provides the easiest method for navigation and learning in a hypertext document.
Graphical	Electronic technologies such as software simulations, product demos, and screen shots have changed the nature of instructional design by taking advantage of the visual representation of information.
Sitemaps	In this respect, a sitemap functions as a visual representation of the entire website from a broad vantage point.
Screen shots	In computer documentation, screen shots act as a type of advance organizer by orienting the user to the application and providing a cognitive context for the information.
Instructional	These advance organizers are either statements that define the expected goal of instructional materials in terms of demonstrable skills or knowledge that will be acquired by a student or a visual representation of a computer screen.
Learning objectives	Instructional materials such as software tutorials often begin with an introductory page that briefly describes the purpose of the tutorial. In addition, there often is a list of contents that enable users to learn in small stages as well as a finished product that provides a mental model.
Screen shots	In computer documentation, screenshots act as a type of advance organizer by orienting the user to the application and providing a cognitive context for the information.

Multimodal	The advent of rich media applications has given rise to an entirely new category of advance organizers. Computer instructional material can now be presented with text, audio, graphics, animation, video, and interactivity.
Product demos and software simulations	Among the most effective of the second-generation advance organizers are product demos and software simulations, which are capable of interactivity and instant feedback and thus facilitate learning by providing higher-level schema. Practice components—interactive controls such as input boxes, checkboxes, and rollovers—require interactivity by the user. The more interactive and repetitive the simulation, the easier it is for the user to acquire and remember a task. Studies have shown that learning improves even more when narration is used in conjunction with software simulations.
Hybrids	Hybrids incorporate product demos and software simulations with a more traditional textual presentation to teach a software application. This uses both a textual preview as well as a software simulation "demo" with a narrator who takes the user through the steps of learning how to add a sound clip to a PDF.

Activity 4.1: Cognitive Theories

Research one of the cognitive theories to better understand it. How do you feel it will impact the format and document design of your technical writing documents? Be prepared to discuss in class.

Credits

Fig. 4.2: Copyright © 2011 Depositphotos/aa-w.

CHAPTER FIVE

Types of Technical Communication Documents

Technical documents tend to fall into broad categories, and readers will have specific expectations of each type of document. This chapter will address the most common types of technical documents that you are likely to encounter professionally and discuss best practices for creating each type of document so that it is most likely to meet the needs of the reader.

CORRESPONDENCE

Purpose

The most common type of technical document you will encounter, both as a reader and a writer, is correspondence. Correspondence falls into three primary categories:

- Email
- Memos
- Letters

Regardless of its form, most correspondence shares characteristics such as:

- Communicating information to one or more readers, who may be internal or external stakeholders
- Addressing one primary message, rather than covering multiple issues in the same document
- Providing an evidentiary trail of events and decisions made

Differing forms of correspondence serve varied functions:

- **Memos (or memoranda)** are internal documents, intended for use inside of an organization. Their structure is less formal than that of a letter, and typically memos are presented in print rather than electronically. Email typically mimics the form of a memo, specifically its heading format of to, from, and so on.
- **Letters** are external documents that are typically presented on company letterhead. While letters are sometimes used internally, especially when dealing with confidential, sensitive information, this level of formality is generally reserved for external stakeholders.
- **Email (electronic mail)** has become the most widely used form of correspondence among both internal and external stakeholders. Email tends to be less formal, and brevity is highly desirable in email communications. In fact, recent studies suggest that readers often will skim the first paragraph of an email and may not read much that follows. Accordingly, you will best meet your readers' needs if you confine email correspondence to short messages. If you have multiple topics to address, consider using separate emails for each topic to ensure that your readers do not miss any of your message.

Correspondence communicates different types of messages. Those messages may include:

- **Good news letters** – Arguably, good news letters are the least complicated to construct, as you are delivering a message that the reader anticipates favorably. Your message can be direct and to the point, often delivered in the first paragraph of the letter.
- **Bad news letters** – Bad news letters, on the other hand, have potential to alienate your readers, although that cannot stop you from delivering relevant news. In delivering bad news, you may find it useful to outline the reasons you cannot agree to the reader's request, and then actually deliver the bad news. Keep in mind that although you may be delivering bad news, you do not want to burn bridges unnecessarily, as down the road you may want to work with the individual again. That being said, attempt to soften the blow without diluting the clarity of the message you need to deliver. In such letters, you may want to consider this type of organization:
    - **1st paragraph** – Try to create goodwill with the reader and generate positive feelings.
    - **2nd paragraph** – Present the bad news as clearly and kindly as possible
    - **3rd paragraph** – Suggest any alternative solutions that might help to resolve the situation in way that is favorable to the reader.
    - **Transmittal letters** – Transmittal letters introduce an accompanying document such as a proposal, feasibility study, or other report-length document. Generally quite short, transmittal letters provide essential context for the

reader as they read the larger document. Transmittal letters will provide a discussion of what is being sent, the reason for sending it, and how to respond to the individual or organization sending the document.

Tone

Regardless of the type of message you deliver with your correspondence, an appropriate tone and attitude are critical to the way in which the reader will receive the message. Your tone will reflect on you, your organization, and the response that your correspondence will earn from the reader. If you assume a tone that accuses the reader of doing something incorrectly or implies that the reader is not paying attention, is being rude, or another negative attribute, the response to your correspondence will most likely be negative and can have a long-term impact on an otherwise good working relationship. Similarly, if you seek to deliver bad news in a clear but non-accusatory manner, you are more likely to earn your reader's cooperation.

Attitude

The attitude of your correspondence reflects the point of view that you have adopted. Often business correspondence spends an inordinate amount of time discussing why a particular message or course of action is beneficial to the writer's organization. While this approach may seem very relevant to the writer, the readers will be most interested in how your message will impact them and their organization. Using a "we" attitude will suggest that you are more interested in your own perspective, while a "you" attitude will suggest that you are looking at the issue from the reader's point of view. Consider the following examples:

> **We** attitude: We ensured that your package was shipped out so it would arrive on time, as we promised.
>
> **You** attitude: You should receive your package by the time you requested it.
>
> **We** attitude: We are sorry to inform you that we cannot increase your credit line at this time.
>
> **You** attitude: Your business is valuable to us, and we regret that we cannot accommodate your request for a credit line increase.

TECHNICAL DESCRIPTIONS

Purpose

Technical descriptions are a common form of technical writing particularly in the technology sector. In addition to engineering specifications, they are part of larger technical documents, including user manuals and marketing literature.

User Manuals

Manufacturers often include an operations manual in the packaging of a mechanism, tool, or piece of equipment. This manual helps users construct, install, operate, and repair the equipment, and technical descriptions in these manuals provide end-users with information about the object's features and capabilities.

Engineering Specifications

Engineering specifications describe the operations and attributes of a product or system while in production. They may be a document, a prototype or mockup, diagrams, or any combination of these.

Sales Literature

Companies use technical descriptions to market equipment or services. Technical descriptions are common in sales materials, feasibility studies, recommendation reports, proposals, and white papers.

TYPES OF TECHNICAL DESCRIPTIONS

Object and Mechanism Descriptions

Object and mechanism technical descriptions are the most common types of technical descriptions. They can describe a single item (object) or a number of items that work together to form a mechanism.

Process Descriptions

Process descriptions describe a sequence of events—each step of how something happens. These differ from instructions, which explain how to do something.

SECTIONAL CONTENT AND CHARACTERISTICS

Introduction — What Is It?

The introduction should explain the type of technical description it is—a process, an object, or a mechanism—and describe its audience and purpose. This first section should also present a broad description of the concept, object, mechanism, or process and outline what you are describing, its functions and capabilities, and its major components. You might also provide a graphic (photograph, screen shot, or drawing) that introduces the readers to the overall concept.

Discussion

Object and Mechanism Discussion — What does it look like?

Object and mechanism technical descriptions may have more than one method of organization:

- **Spatial** – Describes an object or mechanism from top to bottom, bottom to top, left to right, inside to outside, outside to inside, clockwise, or counterclockwise.
- **Functional** – Describes how an object or mechanism works or is used.
- **Chronological** – Describes the process from beginning to end.

To describe the object or mechanism, you may detail the following:

- Composition (materials)
- Weight
- Dimensions
- Shape
- Density
- Color
- Make/model
- Texture
- Capacity

Process Discussion — How does it work and where does it take place?

Process technical descriptions should have these requirements:

- Process descriptions work best when you structure them sequentially.
- You should also explain the causal relationships among the steps—how one step causes or creates the condition for the next step.
- You should always use present tense in your process descriptions.

Conclusion — How does it function?

Object and mechanism technical descriptions typically conclude by briefly stating how the parts function together. Process descriptions conclude by briefly summarizing the main steps of the process.

GRAPHICS

Graphics such as exploded views, photographs, screen shots, and drawings are key to effective technical descriptions. Regardless what type of technical document, you should always discuss the visual before it appears on the page. In addition, ensure that all visuals are descriptively labeled and captioned.

PROPOSALS

Audience Analysis

With a proposal, the most important element is the definition of the problem, situation, or opportunity to which your document is intended to respond. Most readers will toss a proposal aside as soon as they realize that it has not indicated or addressed a particular need.

When you write your proposal, analyze your audience carefully. How can you explain the project so that your readers will understand it? After you have shown that you understand the purpose, describe how you plan to create a document to address it. Convince your readers that you can respond to the situation that you have just described. Above all, the proposal must be persuasive.

Questions Readers Ask

The questions that decision-makers ask when they consider proposals typically concern these topics:

- **Problem** – Your readers will want to know why you are making your proposal and why they should be interested in it. What problem, need, or goal does your proposal address, and why is it important to them?
- **Solution** – Your readers will want to know exactly what you propose to make or do and how it relates to the problem you describe. They will examine your proposal carefully to determine whether your overall strategy and your specific plans are like to work.
- **Time Schedule** – Your readers will want to know specific milestones you will meet to complete your project.
- **Costs** – Your readers will want to know what it will cost to implement your proposal and whether the costs will be worth it to them.
- **Capability** – If your readers authorize you to perform the work, they will want to know that they can depend on you to deliver what you promise.

Basic Structure of Proposals

1. **Introduction — What you propose to do and why the project is important.** You should consider the following structure and information in your introduction:
   - A complete summary of the entire project, showing that you understand the specific purpose.
   - A statement of proposal to create a document to address this situation.
   - An overview of the objectives for your project, each addressing a specific need.

- A brief outline of the goals for your project.
- A list of the benefits if the document is approved.
- Your start and completion dates.

2. **Problems — The project address problem(s), need(s), or goal(s) important to the reader.** Once you've announced what you are proposing, you must persuade your readers that it will address some problem(s), need(s), or goal(s) that is significant to them. Your description of the problem(s) is crucial to the success of your proposal. You must persuade the readers that your proposed project will achieve its objective.

Problem Definition

Convince readers that the proposal addresses a significant problem or need and demonstrate how that problem or need affects them. Persuade them first that a problem or need truly exists and then that it is important to them. Anticipate and answer any questions that readers may have, so they know you clearly understand the situation.

The problem definition should include the following:

- Define the problem in detail.
- Give the background of the problem or situation or explain how it developed. The background may help readers to understand that a significant problem exists or that you understand their needs.
- Explain why the project you propose is necessary. For example, if you are writing a research proposal, explain why the research is important.

Tips for writing the problem definition:

- **Define the problem or need** – Give the readers the details they need to understand the problem(s) or need(s) and why they should then consider your proposed solution or plan of action.
- Present the necessary background for the readers to understand the problem(s) or need(s) and the proposed solution or plan — Give the readers the information they require to understand the context of your proposal.
- Give the readers the information they require to understand why they should approve your proposal — Explain why the proposal is important to the readers.

3. **Objectives — The features will a solution to each problem needs to be successful.** After you describe the problem or need, your writers will want to know how you plan to solve the problem(s) or meet their needs. They will especially want to see a clear link between their problem(s) or needs and your proposed solution. Each problem should be addressed with a corresponding objective, and each goal with a corresponding task.

Tips for writing the objectives section

- Link the proposed solution to the problem by explaining how the solution will solve each problem and meet the needs of the readers – Tell your readers specifically how your proposed solution will solve each problem you describe in the Problem Definition section. Don't assume the readers will see the links. Instead, directly state the link.
- **Explain, in detail, how you plan to do the proposed work** – You want the readers to understand the scope of the work that you are proposing.
- **Present a detailed, step-by-step plan for carrying out the work** – Be sure to justify your plan and to anticipate the readers' possible questions.

4. **Plan of Action** – A sound project management plan that includes the necessary facilities, equipment, and other resources; a workable time schedule; an outline; and all costs. Once you have shown that you understand the needs of the users and have described how you plan to write the document, you discuss your approach to the subject: indicate the elements that you plan to include, the procedures you will follow, and the equipment you will use. You should create a picture of how you will progress from the first day of the project to the last.

Your plan of action should include the following elements:

- A tentative outline of the document in a standard outline format.
- A time schedule (Gantt chart) that outlines the schedule that you plan to follow to create your document.
- A narrative that details each of the milestones and the corresponding dates.

FIGURE 5.1

I. Executive Summary
II. Introduction
III. The Problem of Where to Live
IV. The Problem of Where to Eat
V. Methods of Research
    A. Questionnaires
    B. Surveys
VI. Results
    A. Residence Halls
    B. On-campus Apartments
    C. Off-campus Apartments
    D. Off-campus Houses
VII. Conclusions & Recommendations
VIII. Appendix A: Google Docs Housing Survey

FIGURE 5.2

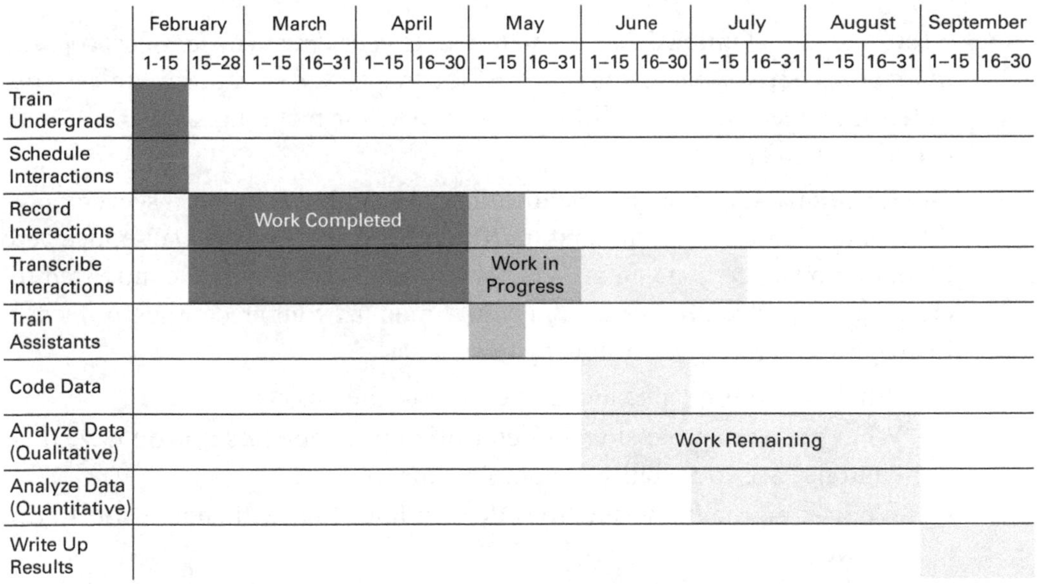

	February		March		April		May		June		July		August		September	
	1-15	15–28	1–15	16–31	1–15	16–30	1–15	16–31	1–15	16–30	1–15	16–31	1–15	16–31	1–15	16–30
Train Undergrads																
Schedule Interactions																
Record Interactions			Work Completed													
Transcribe Interactions							Work in Progress									
Train Assistants																
Code Data																
Analyze Data (Qualitative)											Work Remaining					
Analyze Data (Quantitative)																
Write Up Results																

FIGURE 5.3

Time Schedule/Gantt Chart

Plan of Action

Development Dates: The date ranges below are my expected meeting and editing timeframes.

- **Nov. 10–14:** On these days, I plan to develop the template I have provided to prepare for work. I will meet with you and receive feedback on what information you require in the handbook as well as rules and policies. I will organize this throughout the next period, Nov. 15–21.
- **Nov. 15–21:** We will meet again on one of these days to review the work I have produced and to discuss further what more material is necessary so I may begin to input this material during the next period, Nov. 22–28.
- **Nov. 22–28:** On one of these days, we will work together one last time to finish organizing the information present and fill in the absent information. When you are happy with the information, I will take the next period, Nov. 29- Dec. 2, to edit any errors in typography or style.
- **Nov. 29–Dec. 2:** I will present my finished work to you within this span of time.

5. **Cost Analysis – Optional, but you may donate your time to make your proposal more persuasive.** A budget is optional for this type of proposal, unless you anticipate needing any additional equipment or incurring any additional expenses such as salaries.
6. **Qualifications – Appropriate qualifications to complete the project successfully.** After showing that you understand the readers and have a well-conceived plan, demonstrate that you are the person who is capable and committed to creating the project. In this section, you should list your credentials and work history by answering the following questions:
   - What are your qualifications to carry out the project?
   - What previous professional or educational experiences do you have that demonstrate your ability to complete the project?
   - What equipment and facilities do you have that will enable you to do the work?
7. **Conclusion – Contact information should your reader need it.** Your final paragraph should include your phone number and e-mail address should your reader have questions or would like to discuss the proposal further.

BASIC FORMAT OF PROPOSALS

Informal proposals should be in a memorandum format and include the following elements:

- Sans serif headings and subheadings and serif body text
- Bulleted lists and run-in headings
- A time schedule (Gantt chart) with an accompanying narrative
- Running header with the document title and pagination. Typically, you include the person you are writing to, the page number, and the date in the running head in multi-page correspondence.

Sample Proposal

Memorandum

To: Dr. Kenneth Price

From: Jane Doe

Date: 19 September 2017

Subject: Semester Project Proposal

Introduction

From console, to PC, to handheld, gaming is a staple in today's generation. Not only are classics like Pac-Man and Super Mario Bros still popular, but these traditional games come back in new forms yearly. Online gaming is popular in today's world and it resides at the fingertips of everyone who owns a smartphone. Whatever the platform, gaming continues to bring fun to anyone who plays.

Companies produce new games weekly. They upgrade and remake gaming consoles so as to keep up with the latest technology and heighten the gaming experience. These constant upgrades are a goldmine for people who are just beginning to dive into the gaming world. As newer consoles support the latest games, yesterday's consoles hold still-great games for beginning gamers.

As tempting as it may be to beginners, buying a brand-new gaming console is a bad decision. New consoles are extremely expensive and not worth the dollar if the buyer is just looking for a hobby. So the best decision is to go with cheaper, past generation's consoles. The many platforms and consoles provide another difficult question: which console should you buy?

My project will help readers decide which major console to purchase by comparing and contrasting these consoles. The primary focus for comparing such consoles will be on the physical specifications of each console, the game play experience for the players, and the investment value for each console. Over the next few weeks I will continue my research and analyze my information. I will submit the final project on October 15, 2016.

Problem

Hundreds of gaming forms are on the market right now. Handheld game devices like PS Vita, Nintendo DS, or even smartphone game applications are growing at an alarming rate. PC gaming is always expanding their library. Major corporations like Sony, Microsoft, and Nintendo, are pumping out new and improved consoles yearly. The options are constantly increasing and for a beginning gamer, this growth can be overwhelming.

Focusing on more modern generations, a beginner may boil down their options to two basic and reliable consoles. The two major consoles that are worth considering for beginners are the Sony PlayStation 3 and the Microsoft Xbox 360. Both Sony and Microsoft are tech giants and deciding between them is rather difficult. Both companies provide great gaming experience through their consoles. Both hold equally massive fan bases. If asked, people will usually suggest whatever console they have back at home, giving bias and unhelpful information to beginners.

I went through this decision myself. At first, I made the mistake of asking my friends which console I should purchase. They each claimed the console they owned was by far the better brand. This bias opinion confused me and I decided to follow another direction. I researched and compared resolution outputs, FPS rates, and game controllers. I wanted to decide for myself which console was physically better. I compared prices and game availability as well as console lifespan and online game play. This search allowed me to create an optimal comparison between these two consoles. I am basing my project on these standards.

To decide between these two consoles, the buyer must weigh them against each other in three major ways: physical specifications, game play, and investment value. Buyers comparing these two consoles will have a clear, objective path towards buying their first major gaming console. By following these criteria, buyers will have an easy evaluation method, free from biased opinions of current and past gamers.

Objectives

My semester project will focus on these objectives:

- Compare the physical specifications for the gaming consoles in terms of resolution and FPS output, physical console upgrades, and controller aspects.

- Analyze the online game play and compare the availability of games on the individual consoles.
- Consider the final investment value of each console in terms of energy usage, lifespan, and cost.

Editing

I will meet with my classmates this Monday (9/19/16) to edit my proposal. I will reference online material to ensure I write in the correct format. I will edit the project proposal and the project on the week days. I will have the project reviewed by my professor. I will continue to edit the final project in the week and throughout the weekend. I will edit the final project before submitting it in online.

Plan of Action

Since my professor approved my topic, I will begin to research my topic in more detail. I will consolidate my past experiences into notes and begin integrating them into a first draft. I will have it reviewed by my peers, and I will edit the project appropriately.

I will continue my research online by visiting both Microsoft and Sony's websites and investigating each console's specifications. I will also continue my research by performing tests on both consoles and recording data on their performance. I will continue this research and revise my project report until the due date of October 15, 2016.

After my peer editors review my project and I correct it, I will begin the rough draft and continue to edit the material. I will have my peers review the project and edit it accordingly. I will then ask my professor to review it, and I will edit it accordingly. After my final draft is complete, I will save it on a PDF format and post it on Blackboard. Table I presents the schedule for my project.

TABLE I: Time Schedule

	0 DAYS	10 DAYS	20 DAYS	30 DAYS
Research	9/20/16–10/14/16			
Draft Project		9/26/16–10/3/16		
Peer Edit Project		10/3/16–10/9/16		
Conference with Professor			10/10/16–10/12/16	
Final Edit Project				10/13/16–10/14/16
Submit Final Project				10/15/16

Development Dates

The dates described below correspond with table I.

- **Sept. 19:** I will take the rough draft of my proposal and have it reviewed by three of my peers. I will continue editing this proposal until Sept. 25.
- **Sept. 20–Oct. 14:** I will continue my research by playing games on both consoles, reading product descriptions online, and collecting data on the consoles. I will continue to do this research till Oct. 15.
- **Sept. 20–Sept. 25:** This week, I will take it to my professor and he will review the proposal. I will edit it accordingly.
- **Sept. 25:** I will convert my final proposal into PDF format. I will upload the final proposal into Blackboard.
- **Sept. 26–Oct. 3:** I will formulate the rough draft of my project. I will gather my information and begin writing the first rough draft of my semester project.
- **Oct. 3–Oct. 9:** I will bring the rough draft of my final project to class. My peer editing group will edit my project rough draft. I will revise the paper accordingly.
- **Oct. 10–Oct. 12:** I will bring the rough draft of my final project to my professor. My professor will review my project rough draft.
- **Oct. 13–Oct. 14:** On these two days, I will edit my project in response to my peer's and professor's reviews. I will edit the final parts of my project.
- **Oct. 15:** I will convert my final project into PDF format. I will upload the final project into Blackboard.

The format of my report will be similar to the format in this proposal. The final project will be 10-12 pages in length. The project will use Calibri 14 pt. for headings and Cambria 12 pt. body text. I will use comparison charts and tables to better analyze my project's objectives.

The following is a working outline of my feasibility/recommendation report:

I. Abstract/Summary

II. Introduction

  A. Problems

  B. Objectives

III. Research

  A. Console Specifications

    1. Resolution and FPS Output

    2. Console Upgrades

    3. Controller Aspects

   B. Game Play
      1. Online Game Play
      2. Available Games
   C. Investment Value
      1. Energy Usage
      2. Lifespan
      3. Costs

IV. Evaluation
   A. Individual consoles
   B. Criteria

V. Conclusion and Personal Reference

VI. Index

VII. References

Cost Analysis

This project will have no costs. I have direct access to Microsoft Word and free access to online resources and university resources. I will use my own equipment at no cost.

Qualifications

I am qualified to do this project because I have decided between these two consoles myself. I researched both consoles on the internet and in person. I also have personal experience with each console, and I use both consoles regularly. I know what people will look for in a console because I have done so myself.

This project report will be credible because I analyze these consoles daily. I have past and current experiences that qualify me for performing a detailed comparison of such gaming consoles.

Conclusion

This report will provide a direct method when choosing between these two consoles. While both consoles have their advantages and disadvantages, the decision will be less stressful due to the information I will provide in this report. I know that buyers will decide between these two consoles, and I believe that with this report, they will find the decision easier to make. For any further discussion or analyzation of these two consoles, please call my personal phone at (215) 555-0584. To schedule a meeting or to continue debate about buying one of these two consoles, email me at leigh.jones@students.tamuk.edu.

Progress (or Status) Reports

Technical writers typically create regular status reports to update project managers and team members on how projects you are involved with are progressing.

Organization

A progress or status report is organized around the answers to the following questions:

- **What time period does this report cover?**
  Progress reports are most commonly weekly, but are organized around project milestones established by a project manager.
- **What are the objectives of the project?**
  This information is commonly detailed in the original project specifications or project proposal.
- **What have you accomplished so far?**
  Here you summarize the progress you have made on the project goals you summarized in the Objectives section.
- **What work remains to be done?**
  You may use an infographic or a Gantt chart to highlight milestones, then track how the team has progressed toward achieving them.
- **What problems have you encountered?**
  Here you detail any issues that have come up since the last progress report.
- **What changes do you recommend to the project?**
  How will these changes affect the overall progress of the project? If you recommend the project change, such as extending the schedule or revising the requirements, you open a change request.

Format

What is the project that you are reporting about? This is answered with project identifiers:

- Project name
- Project ID/code
- Name of project manager
- Date of report

A progress report has three main sections:

- Introduction/Overview
- Discussion of progress of the project
- Conclusion

Introduction/Overview

The first section should identify the document as a progress report, as well as state the time period of the work that the report covers. For example, the report may be the second of fourth, or it may be a weekly or bi-weekly status report. In addition, the report should name the project that the work covers and state the objectives of the project.

Discussion of the Progress

Describes in detail the work you have accomplished and the progress you have made during this phase of the project.

Progress and status reports typically follow two methods of organization:

- Work Accomplished/Progress Expected
- Task Organization

Regardless of the method you choose, you should be careful to define the project tasks clearly.

Work Accomplished/Progress Expected

Work Accomplished

- Task 1
- Task 2
- Task 3

Progress Expected

- Task 1
- Task 2
- Task 3

Task Organization

Task 1
- Work Accomplished
- Progress Expected

Task 2
- Work Accomplished
- Progress Expected

Conclusion

Your discussion may conclude with a revised timeline (Gantt Chart) that details where you are in the project in relation to where you thought you would be. The conclusion evaluates the overall progress on the project. If you have experienced problems, particularly those that have you behind schedule, mention them here, but be sure to show how you havc solved them. End with your phone number and email address.

Sample Progress Report

Memorandum

Date: March 26, 2018

To: Dr. Kenneth Price

From: Amanda Holmes

Subject: English 303 Comprehensive Edit Progress Report

Overview

Black Box Network Services is a world-leader in comprehensive communications and infrastructure solutions with the largest footprint in the industry and over 175,000 clients in every major industry sector. One of the first interactions clients have with Black Box Network Services is to read the company's capabilities statement. The capabilities statement for the Federal Government branch of the company currently is lacking pertinent information and does not represent the company to the fullest extent possible.

For my semester project, I am editing the capabilities statement for the Federal Government branch of Black Box Network Services. The updated capabilities statement will conform to the company's Style Guide, will have a more thorough capabilities section, and will have a more reader-friendly Past Performances section. The readers of this document will be potential and existing customers of the Federal Government branch of Black Box Network Services.

This memorandum provides an update on the tasks completed since the project proposal was submitted on Monday, March 12, 2012, and the expected progress of the editing project. I anticipate completing the entire project by Friday, April 13, 2012.

Work Accomplished and Progress Expected

In my proposal, I explained the primary editing objectives for this project: conforming the document to the style guide of Black Box Network Services, extending the capabilities section, converting the entire document into an editable format, and creating a more reader-friendly past performances section. For the purposes of this progress report, I have listed the original goals as tasks and, in the following section, I explain the work that has been accomplished as well as the expected progress of the project.

Task 1: Conform Document to Style Guide

When the original capabilities statement was drafted, the author was new to Black Box Network Services and was unfamiliar with the company's Style Guide.

- Work Accomplished - I have changed the document's color palette so that it is in line with the company's official colors. I have changed the font of the text, subheadings, and headlines to the approved font family for electronic media and media created on a PC device. I have removed all the instances of passive voice and inserted serial commas where necessary. I have changed the capitalization of headlines so that they are in sentence style rather than headline style.
- Progress Expected - I need to check and see if any trademarks or registered trademarks are used so that they can be properly noted.

Task 2: Extend Capabilities Section

The capabilities section should comprise the majority of the capabilities document, but at present, it is only one-third of the total document's length. I wanted to expand the capabilities section so that it was more comprehensive and comprised a larger section of the document.

- Work Accomplished - I have performed preliminary research of the company and the work that it does in order to find information that could be included in the capabilities section of the document.
- Progress Expected - I still need to organize the information that I intend to add to the capabilities statement and actually incorporate it into the document. I also need to update the Table of Contents to reflect this information.

Task 3: Convert Entire Document into an Editable Format

A large portion of the capabilities section of the document is comprised of JPG images that have been copied from the company website. This current format makes it difficult for someone to edit the document. My goal was to remove the JPGs and re-enter the information as text blocks.

- Work Accomplished – I have converted the Who We Serve section of the document from a JPG image into an editable text format.
- Progress Expected – I still need to re-enter the information for the Data Infrastructure, Voice Communications, and Products sections of the document as well as the second page of the Footprint section.

Task 4: Create a More Reader-Friendly Past Performances Section

The Past Performances section provides readers with a better understanding of how Black Box will be able to handle their telecommunications needs by providing them with previous examples of work performed by Black Box. This section of the document should be engaging, and it is my goal to edit this portion of the document so that it holds the reader's attention until the end.

- Work Accomplished – I have spoken with my contact person and requested more information regarding the specific past performances mentioned so as to try and find a better way to format the information rather than in long paragraphs.
- Progress Expected – I still need to change the format of the Ft. Bragg, North Carolina; State of Tennessee; and White Oak, Maryland, past performance descriptions. I intend to incorporate run-in headings and bulleted lists and to shorten the length of the paragraphs.

Conclusion

When I created my initial timeline for this project, I did not consider the projects I would be working on for other classes as well. As such I have not been able to accomplish as much as I had initially thought was possible. My conference is scheduled for Wednesday, March 28, at which point I will meet with my instructor to discuss the current status of the project. By the end of the week I will finish re-entering the information that is currently in JPG format. I will spend one week each editing the Capabilities section and Past Performances section of the document before I submit it Friday, April 13.

Credits

Fig. 5.2: Copyright © by Microsoft.

CHAPTER SIX

Writing for the Technology Industry

COMPUTER DOCUMENTATION

USER PROFILES AND TASK ANALYSES

One of the most common types of technical writing is for the technology sector. Computer documentation specialists use a variety of instructional media to help users learn and become proficient with a particular program. Since the type of documentation depends in large part on what the end-users know about a product, these begin with the most basic steps and move toward more advanced tasks.

Instructions are often written by people who have a vast amount of experience with an application, object, or process. These experts sometimes become too familiar with how to perform the tasks and have difficulty describing the information to a novice user.

Audience profiles inform the goals and objectives of technical publications. Audience analysis is one of the most widely accepted parts of the planning process and one of the least effectively performed. A simple truth about audience analysis is that without a clear picture of the end-user who will be reading and using a document, the technical writer is unlikely to design a document that meets the audience's needs. There simply is no way to construct this picture without extensive audience profiles.

Determine how much information your user needs

You may design procedures of varying detail, depending upon the difficulty of the task or the reader's experience. You will gather this information from questionnaires, surveys, and user profiling and task analyses. A publications staff cannot produce sound goals and objectives until they understand the users, the environment in which they must work, and the tasks that they want to perform.

Audience Profiles

Every documentation plan must contain an audience profile based on fact rather than opinion. The most common flaw is to assume that the user is exactly the same as the technical writer. It is essential that the writer survey, interview, and observe members of the target audience directly to get a clear picture of who the audience is.

PERSONAS

One common practice for user profiling in professional communication is by creating personas, or audience composites. Personas involve creating profiles for a small number of archetypal users, each profile representing a composite of a group of users. Information for the profiles is derived from user interviews, reviews of market research and customer feedback, and statistics about how a product is used.

The number of personas need not be large, with no more than three primary personas representing the primary target audience and up to four secondary personas when the needs of the user population are extensive.

Create Audience Composites

Each persona is typically represented with a photograph, name, description, and details about specific interests and relevant behaviors. It is often useful for members of the design, development, and usability testing teams to role-play different personas. This is an effective means of seeing something from the user's perspective. Personas not only make the target audience more real to designers and engineers, they also ensure that requirements are prioritized to specifically meet the users' needs.

Define User Characteristics in Personas

Describe the background of the users. Include pertinent information, such as educational level and skills, experience with technology, and job responsibilities.

TABLE 6.1

	ANDY	ROBERT	SID

Age	9	59	63
Occupation	Elementary student	Accountant	Corn/wheat farmer
Education	4th Grader	MBA	High School Diploma

TABLE 6.1 (continued)

	ANDY	ROBERT	SID
Web Usage	Uses the web for learning/typing games.	Uses the internet daily for work correspondence, research, and emailing grandchildren.	Uses the internet for news and social media.
Reason for using Fun 4 the Brain	Learning and playing games at home.	Monitoring the websites his grandchildren frequent.	FaceTimes with his grandchildren online.

Task Analyses

Once the writer has profiled the users, one method of creating a task analysis is to begin with a narrative that focuses upon these characteristics:

- Situation
- Name
- Decision
- Steps
- Result

TABLE 6.2

CHARACTERISTICS	INFORMATION FOR CREATING THE TASK ANALYSIS
Situation	Who usually performs this task When they need to perform a certain task
Name	What the user calls the task
Decision	Scale of the task Frequency the user performs the task Whether the task is part of a sequence of other large-scale tasks
Steps	Step-by-step process to complete the task
Result	Whether the task been successfully carried out How the screen appears after the process is complete

Usability Goals

You should set usability goals in the initial stages of the documentation process. Once you determine which goals you would like to see accomplished, you can test how effectively you've met these needs during the usability testing phase of the documentation process. Usability goals stress the importance of making your document as usable as possible under the conditions that you identify in the user profile and task analysis. Usability goals provide the basis for later usability testing. You should set your goals early to later be able to judge whether they have been adequately accomplished.

For example, the usability goals might include the following:

- Participants will be able to download and install the application in 15 minutes or less, with no assistance.
- Participants will be able to begin using the application with no documentation.
- Participants will be able to complete activities or locate specific information within specific time limits.

LEARNING PATHS

Once you create a comprehensive user profile, you can begin to understand the users' learning paths, which is the typical progression that the end-user follows to develop expertise with a tool or application. Learning paths can be any combination of information and its delivery, from reference material, to online and print training, to user forums.

TABLE 6.3

Instructional Materials Specific to the Technology Sector	
Visual Quick Start	Takes beginners by the hand and shows them what the product can do with only the briefest explanations of key concepts and abbreviated procedures for fundamental tasks.
Tutorials	Shows beginners exactly how to do basic typical tasks with the product while learning their way around the program. These need not cover every program feature, just the most common ones.
Procedures	Provides step-by-step instructions for using the product, addressing the fuller range of tasks that the user might want to do.
Command Reference	Lists all of the commands, along with their menus, icons, dialog boxes, keyboard shortcuts, choices, and options.
Onscreen Help	Puts useful information such as procedures, command reference, and keyboard shortcuts on the screen for a user to see while working with the software.
Quick Reference Card	Prompts users how to carry out key steps of procedures or, at the very least, offers a map showing all possible menus and commands.

Writing Procedures

Instructions are often written by people who have a vast amount of experience with an application, object, or process. These experts sometimes become too familiar with how to perform the tasks and have difficulty describing the information to a novice user.

TABLE 6.4

Elements of Procedures	
Task	The task name identifies the program function in performance-oriented language. The task name should describe what job the user performs, not what functions they use. These are often set off with a different predetermined typeface or rule. Using the save function (Weak) Saving a file (Strong)
Scenario	An advance organizer in narrative form should tell the reader what the task will allow them to achieve. Mention here if the user needs a particular skillset to perform the task.
Steps	Steps are numbered and sequentially ordered in vertical lists.
Elaborations	Elaborations explain the steps, commenting on them as they are performed. The writer often provides the following information in elaborations: • Possible mistakes and how to avoid them • How to perform procedures more efficiently • Alternative keystrokes, toolbars, or function keys • Definitions of terms • Ways to tell if the user has performed a step correctly • Where else to look for additional information
Tables	Use tables when you have to include a list of commands or keystrokes. Put this type of information in a table, and be sure to cite the table in the text.

COGNITIVE THEORIES ASSOCIATED WITH INSTRUCTIONAL MATERIAL

TABLE 6.5

Perceived structure	We seek and use visual structure to skim and scan information quickly for relevant information. Our perceptual system is influenced by these factors. We perceive what we expect, and our expectations are formed by three factors: • Our past experiences • The current context • Our goals and plans for the future. We tend to filter things unrelated to our goals.
Chunking	First put forward in the 1950s by George A. Miller, a Harvard psychologist. He published a landmark study of short-term memory entitled "The Magical Number Seven, Plus or Minus Two." The chunking principle suggests the number (channel capacity) that people could be reliably expected to remember a few minutes after having been told these numbers only once. Chunking limits are the result of research that indicates the average person can process and remember an amount of information based on the media and complexity of the information. For online documents, this number is even smaller.
Channel Capacity	The amount of space in the human brain for certain kinds of information. This is the reason that the telephone number is seven digits. Bell wanted the number to be as long as possible. But time and time again, tests have shown this natural limit of intellectual capacity. Writers should classify the information into smaller logically related groups and introduce a subheading.
Advance Organizers	Depending upon the type of instructions, you may want to provide some type of overview or summary. This may include the amount of time, tools, source files, or experience necessary to accomplish the task.

WRITING STYLES

The writing style used in instructions depends upon the experience level of the user.

Elaborative Writing

Elaborative documentation is an approach to teaching technology skills that includes summaries, explanations, examples, and articulations of goals and objectives. While summaries and overviews may distract the user from focusing upon information, these elements help users to apply their tasks to real-world situations.

Minimalist Writing

Minimalist writing requires a detailed needs assessment and extensive user. Moreover, the minimalist writing approach needs more thorough usability testing.

Strategies for writing minimalistic computer documentation include the following:

1. Use task-oriented titles, headings, and subheadings rather than lengthy introductions to lists. Relate the headings to the tasks that the users perform.
2. Use a common structure, so users know what to expect before they begin the procedure.
3. Use "chunking." Have small chunks that the reader can see, understand, and follow at a glance.
4. Use a hierarchical format with outlines and lists. Visual queuing—point size, typography, white space—will help the user to follow the document.
5. Use indicators that differentiate between what to do, how to do it, and other information types.
6. Rely on visuals (especially screen shots and callouts). Documents written for the computer industry are graphic-intensive.
7. Use clear, task-oriented tables of contents and well-constructed indices.
8. Review online material online. This reduces the size of the document.
9. Create documentation with minimal punctuation.
10. Extensively usability-test the documentation.

Particularly with procedures, use-structured or modular writing, action- and task-oriented headings and subheadings, and numbered sequential steps, have consistent user orientation devices such as colors, fonts, and typefaces to show the hierarchy of the document or screen.

FORMATTING AND STRUCTURING PROCEDURES

Step Format

For most types of instructions, the step format is most appropriate. This format enables users to follow the information in an organized fashion. When you write using the step format, keep the number of steps in the procedure small. Individuals with cognitive impairments may have difficulty following multi-step procedures. Research has shown that most procedures should be no more than seven steps but having fewer is better, especially with online computer documentation such as help systems.

Style

TABLE 6.6

STYLE	
Active voice	**Rather than** Discussion boards, blogs, tests, and assignments can also be built outside of the Learning Modules. **Use** You can build discussion boards, blogs, tests, and assignments outside of the learning modules. **Rather than** Before proceeding any further, make sure the server is stopped. **Use** Before proceeding any further, stop the server.
Imperative mood	The imperative mood is typical of instructions. The actor is the understood "You" or second person. Imperative mood sentences often begin with a verb. The highlighted verbs in the following sentences are in the imperative mood: **Enter** the name of the Learning Module. **Close** the dialog box.
Parallel structure	Parallel structure means using the same pattern of words to show that two or more ideas have the same level of importance. This can be a word, phrase, or clause. The usual way to join parallel structures is with coordinating conjunctions such as "and" or "or." **Not Parallel:** Mary likes hiking, swimming, and to ride a bicycle. **Parallel:** Mary likes hiking, swimming, and riding a bicycle. **Not Parallel:** The production manager was asked to write his report quickly, accurately, and in a detailed manner. **Parallel:** The production manager was asked to write his report quickly, accurately, and thoroughly.

Structure

TABLE 6.7

STRUCTURE	FOR INSTRUCTIONS USING A STEP FORMAT, FOLLOW THESE GUIDELINES.
Have only one step per number	**Rather than** 1. Click **Breaks**, and then click **Next Page**. **Use** 1. Click Breaks. 2. Click Next Page.
Number steps only, not results	**Rather than** 1. On the page after the section break, double-click in the header or footer area where you want to display page numbers. 2. Word opens the header or footer for editing and automatically displays the **Header & Footer** tab. **Use** 1. On the page after the section break, double-click in the header or footer area where you want to display page numbers. 2. Word opens the header or footer for editing and automatically displays the **Header & Footer** tab. **Rather than** 1. Click Submit to save. 2. You will be returned to the Content Page. **Use** 1. Click Submit to save. 2. You will be returned to the Content Page.
For steps with options, use a bulleted list	Do one of the following: • To link to an anchor named "top" in the current document, type #top. • To link to an anchor named "top" in a different document in the same folder, type "filename. html# top."
Provide directions for both Windows and Mac users	1. Control-click (Windows) or Command-click (Mac) to select several columns.
Avoid directional terms	Avoid directional terms (left, right, up, down) if possible. Individuals with cognitive impairments may have difficulty interpreting them as do blind users relying upon screen readers.

To usability test for effective instructional material, create a document with no text, just visuals only. Then try a version without visuals. With only one method, can your readers still figure out what to do?

NARRATIVE FORMAT

For some types of instructions, a narrative format is more appropriate, such as the following example:

Proofing Your Design

Unless you're using a photograph, verify that your design contains only spot colors. Choose File > Print. Select the Output pane, and choose Separations (Host-Based) from the Mode menu. In the Document Ink Options area, a printer icon appears next to each ink that will print. Make sure that all your spot inks are listed and that a printer icon doesn't appear next to any of the process colors (marked with a four-color icon). To print a proof, change the Mode to Composite and print the design to a standard printer. Remember that the colors may look different on paper than they will on fabric.

TABLE 6.8

PORTFOLIO BUILDER 6.1 – INSTRUCTION CRITIQUE

REQUIREMENTS

The requirements for the instruction critique are the following:

1. Find a set of instructions that you think is poorly written.
2. Using the Guidelines for Critiquing the Instructions below, evaluate the instructions and decide what needs to be rewritten/redesigned.
3. Write a 2 to 4-page memorandum that evaluates the original set of instructions, as well as a brief summary of and the rationale for the improvements you would make.

GUIDELINES FOR CRITIQUING THE INSTRUCTIONS

Use the following questions as guidelines for critiquing the instructions:

FORMAT

Introduction

1. Do the instructions have an effective advance organizer?
2. Does the introduction state the purpose of the task?
3. Does the introduction list any knowledge or necessary tools or materials the user should have?

CONCLUSION

1. Does the conclusion include any necessary follow-up advice?
2. Does the conclusion include a trouble-shooting guide?

ORGANIZATION

1. Is the instruction set organized in task-oriented, sequential steps?
2. Is the set constructed with a deductive framework (i.e., general to specific)?
3. Are instructions (such as user actions) clearly separate from system reactions?

DESIGN

1. Are there sufficient user cues? User cues include the following:
    - **Textual cues:** tables of contents, indices, overviews, introductions, conclusions, summaries, etc.
    - **Page format cues**: numbers, bullets, tabs, color, headings, running headers or footers, indentations, capitals, typeface, boxes, rules, columns, icons, white space, etc.
2. Is the information chunked appropriately? Or is the information dense and difficult to navigate through?

STYLE

1. Do the instructions use active voice? Rather than, "The bolt is placed on top," the instruction should read, "Place the bolt on top."
2. Does the set of instructions use precise action verbs, such as "place," "connect," "click," and "type"?
3. Are the steps numbered and indented?
4. Is any part of the instructions ambiguous or difficult to understand?
5. Are the instructions written with parallel structure?
6. Are the instructions numbered?
7. Do the instructions use imperative mood?
8. Do the instructions have only one step per number?

GRAPHICS

1. Do the instructions have a clear relationship between the graphics and the accompanying text?
2. Are appropriate graphics included?
3. Are any and all graphics and diagrams clearly labeled and explained in the text?

SCREEN SHOTS

Screen captures focus the user on the events on the screen. Include screen captures when the user needs either to see the tool to use or the results of an action.

- Show the partial result of the procedure to help the reader keep on track.
- Show the final result of the procedure to let the user know when the procedure ends.
- Show dialog boxes where the user has to make choices.
- Show toolbars to indicate which the tools the user needs.
- Show menus to indicate the commands the user needs.

CALLOUTS

Callouts are a textual element of a drawing that clarify the illustration and provide readers with additional information or instructions. They alert readers to specific details of a drawing and conceptually connect the drawing to the text it illustrates.

CREATING CALLOUTS

Because some online document viewers cannot display callouts that are not part of the document, callouts often need to be created within the graphic itself and then imported into the document. When you write the text for callouts, keep the terms and descriptions simple, concise, and consistent. Address only the elements of the drawing you are discussing in the related text.

TABLE 6.9

TYPES OF CALLOUTS	
Tag-style Callouts	Tag-style callouts are the most common. This callout style begins with a capital letter, followed by all lowercase letters. Check MSP for Figure placement

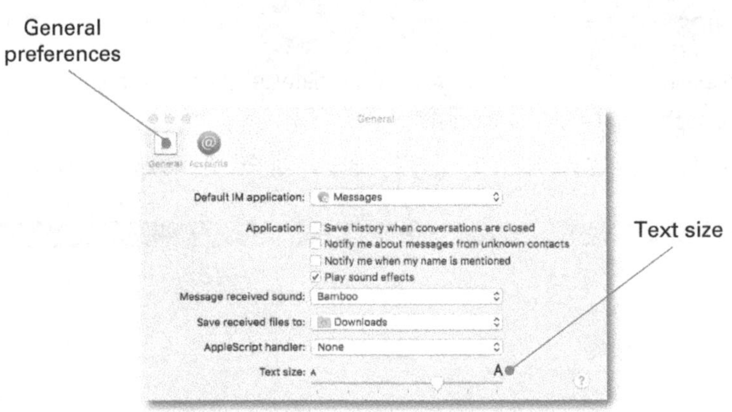

TABLE 6.9 (continued)

TYPES OF CALLOUTS

Sentence-style Callouts

Sentence-style callouts are in the form of a full sentence with terminal punctuation. Keep these callouts short and simple. Translated sentences can be much longer than the original, so leave extra room to keep it from interfering with the drawing.

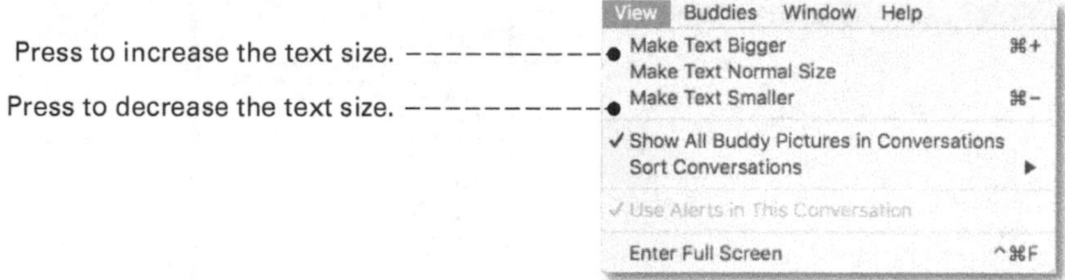

Legends and Notes

Legends and notes have the same specifications as tag-style callouts. Position them approximately 1/2 inch below the drawing when possible.

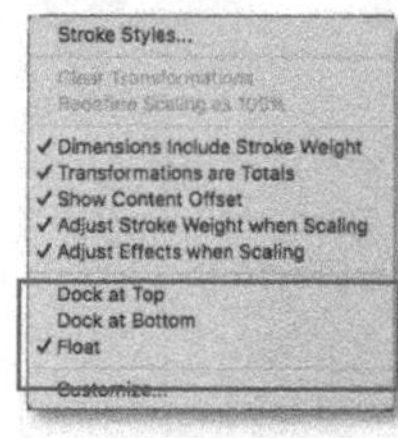

Control Palette
For quick access to many formatting and positioning controls, use the Control Palette, which is at the top of the screen by default. The Control palette is context-sensitive; it's basically three palettes in one. When you have the Type, tool selected, the Control palette offers text-formatting options: character-level formatting options when the A is selected A, and paragraph-level formatting options when the ¶ is selected B. When you use any other tool, the Control palette offers positioning and transformation options C.

Headings

Use headings to title objects or groups of objects and to show sequential events, such as instructions. Headings do not have leader lines. To show sequences, label alphabetically with capital letters and right parentheses, followed by the description. If you are not showing a sequence, you can place headings beneath the objects they describe.

Memory module

TABLE 6.9 (continued)

TYPES OF CALLOUTS	
Aligning Callouts	Line up callouts either vertically or horizontally. Flush left is the most common method of aligning callout type. When possible, keep callouts aligned left and placed to the left of the screen capture, but do not use them to crowd too many callouts to one side. 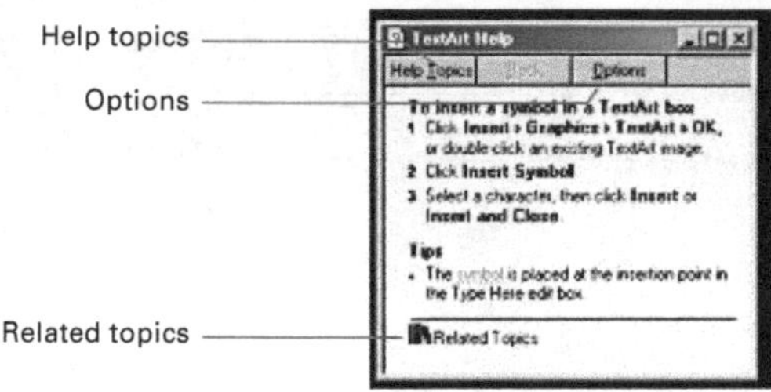
Leader Lines	Place callouts inside an object, but when in doubt, place callouts outside an object. If your document will be translated, place outside whenever possible. Do not use leaders in illustrations depicting a general idea.

Sizing Callouts

For clarity, a rule of thumb for standard callout size is no greater than 1.75 inches wide and four lines of text deep.

If your callout is longer than this, try rewriting it by breaking the information into more than one callout or by putting the information into a note or legend.

SINGLE-CHAPTER TECHNICAL MANUALS

Technical manuals are typically classified as being one of two types:

- Single-chapter manuals
- Multiple-chapter manuals

Single-Chapter Manuals

Manuals with a single chapter are typically small and narrowly focused on a single subject.

Examples

- Simple installation manuals
- Release notes
- White papers
- Readme files

RELEASE NOTES

Purpose

Release notes are a collection of up-to-the-last-minute information on a particular release of a product that alert customers to the changes in a software product with a new release. They decrease calls to support personnel by providing last-minute product information so that customers can easily and quickly install and use a released product and provide customers with exclusive information that is so recent it is not found elsewhere.

Scope

Typically, the information included in a release note relates to installing and using a particular "release" of a software. A company produces a release note as a cost-effective means to quickly convince customers that late-breaking issues related to a product are either not serious or have been fixed.

Customers use a release note to determine if they want to upgrade to a new product release. If they do upgrade to the new release, customers then use the release note to install the product correctly and to get up-to-date information on new features as well as past and present issues with using the release.

Audience

The typical audience of a release note includes engineering, support, and administrative personnel, including:

- Customer application engineers, design engineers, sales engineers, and test engineers
- System administrators, system integrators, technicians
- Support personnel

Distribution Schedule

A company issues technical release notes as closely as possible to the product's release date to ensure the most up-to-date information is included. Because of the last-minute nature of the information included in a technical release note, it is often too late to incorporate this information into a product manual. As a result, typical ways to distribute a technical release note are via email attachment or PDF download.

Distribution Format

Typically release notes are distributed in a format that can be read on any operating system, across any platform: ASCII, HTML, or PDF. Release notes in PDF and HTML formats allow graphics to be included, and a PDF file is also highly searchable and may include hyperlinked terms, such as an index, to relevant sections.

TABLE 6.10

RELEASE NOTES COMPONENTS	
Identification of the product and release	Name Date Version (Release) number
What's new in the product	About the release New features and changes to the product Improvements to the product Problems corrected Support resources: Documentation Tutorials Forums
Improvements in performance and stability	Major changes/updates, Issues addressed, Crashes addressed, Bugs addressed
Known issues	Information about known issues that exist in this version of the product: Installation issues Platform issues Operational issues
Updates to help and documentation	Last-minute changes and corrections to errata Types of documentation Product manuals Tutorials/lessons Help Media available Printable PDFs HTML Help files
Links to bug report and feature request forms	Links to feature request and bug report forms Send features users would like to see in future versions of an application. Alert a company about bugs found in the software to improve a product.
Notices, terms, conditions, and attribution	Third-party software notices Additional terms and conditions as described for each product Notices and/or additional terms and conditions that are part of a product's End-User License Agreement

README FILES

A Readme file is a short, written document distributed with a piece of software. A Readme file accompanies a product and contains information the user needs to read before installing or using the product.

Written by the software's developers, Readme files contain basic, crucial information about the software, including installation or configuration instructions, contact information, licensing information, acknowledgements, and information about the software version.

A Readme file contains information about other files in a directory or archive and is commonly included with computer software. It is traditionally written in uppercase so that on case-preserving environments using an ASCII ordering, the name will appear near the beginning of a directory listing (since uppercase letters sort before lowercase letters in ASCII ordering). Usually Readme files are in plain text or Rich Text Format to prevent formatting issues when opening or reading the file.

House Style Guides for Readme Files

Larger companies may have a house style guide for Readme files, for example:

Here is a summary of the preferred format:

- Headings in all caps.
- Headings underlined with ===/--- to the length of the heading, followed by a newline.
- Two lines between headings (except the first).
- Bullets denoted by asterisks (*) with hanging indents.
- Numbered lists indented four spaces.
- Bulleted lists indented one space.

Readme files can have the same sections as a technical report's front matter.

TABLE 6.11

FRONT MATTER
INCLUDE THESE ELEMENTS AT THE BEGINNING OF THE FILE.

Element	Format	Sample
Titles	Use the document's name enclosed in quotation marks.	READ BEFORE YOU INSTALL [*PRODUCT NAME*]
	For Readme files containing information other than "before you install," use the name "about product name."	ABOUT [*PRODUCT NAME*]
	Another option is to center the publication information.	---------------------------- dBase Wizardry 5 Readme File January 2017 ©2013-2017 TexTech Solutions. All rights reserved. ----------------------------

TABLE 6.11 (continued)

FRONT MATTER INCLUDE THESE ELEMENTS AT THE BEGINNING OF THE FILE.		
Contents	Provide a table of contents of at least one level that lists all the section headings. Order the Readme file with the most important information first. Section numbers are optional	--------- CONTENTS --------- 1. WHAT'S NEW IN THIS RELEASE 2. INSTALLATION NOTES 3. KNOWN BUGS 4. TROUBLESHOOTING
Elements	The contents typically include one or more of the following elements: • Contact information for the distributor or programmer • Brief description • Configuration instructions • Installation instructions • Operating instructions • A file manifest (list of files included) • Known bugs and instructions on how to report new ones • Troubleshooting • Credits and acknowledgments • A detailed changelog intended for programmers • A "News" changelog intended for users • Copyright and licensing information	

PORTFOLIO BUILDER 6.2 – RELEASE NOTES AND README FILES

Find a set of release notes or a Readme file online. Write a short memo that evaluates the content and format. Describe the target audience of the document. How relevant and/or useful do you think the information is? What information would you include or exclude?

Credits

Table 6.1a: Copyright © 2017 Depositphotos/IgorVetushko.
Table 6.1b: Copyright © 2012 Depositphotos/mangostock.
Table 6.1c: Copyright © 2012 Depositphotos/Boguslavovna.
Table 6.9a: Copyright © by Apple, Inc.
Table 6.9b: Copyright © by Apple, Inc.
Table 6.9c: Copyright © by Adobe Systems Incorporated.
Table 6.9d: Copyright © by Adobe Systems Incorporated.
Table 6.9e: Copyright © 2015 Depositphotos/belchonock.
Table 6.9f: Copyright © by Corel Corporation.

CHAPTER SEVEN

Research in Technical Communication

Most research in technical communication is empirical, drawn from primary sources, and different from a research paper for a science class or an argumentative paper in a freshman composition class, which rely primarily upon secondary sources. Primary sources include questionnaires and surveys, interviews, results of experiments, lectures and speeches, and statistical data gathered from usability tests. A secondary source of information is one that is created by someone who did not experience first-hand or participate in the events.

USABILITY TESTING

A common method of research in technical communication, particularly in the technology industry, is usability testing. Usability refers to the user's experience when interacting with products or systems, including websites, software, devices, or applications.

Usability testing is a process in which people who are representative of the intended users of a product are asked to use the product or its information before the product is released to the public. In this way you can address problems you identify in the test before your company releases a product.

Usability is not a single property of a product, system, or user interface. Usability is about effectiveness, efficiency, and the overall satisfaction of the user. When measuring usability, you should look at these metrics:

- **Intuitive** – Being able to almost effortlessly work though the architecture and navigation of a technical document.
- **Easy to learn** – How quickly a user who has never seen technical documentation can accomplish basic tasks.
- **Efficient** – How quickly an experienced user can accomplish tasks using the documentation.

- **Error frequency and severity** – How often users make errors while using the system, how serious the errors are, and how users recover from the errors.
- **Subjective satisfaction** – Whether the user likes to use the material.

Other benefits that can arise from sound and effective usability testing include creating data from which to measure future modifications of a document, minimizing calls to customer support, reducing risk, and increasing sales rates. Ultimately usability testing allows consumers to find potential pitfalls and suggests improvements before the product is made available to the public.

The key to effective usability testing is to establish research objectives. Are you interested in attitudes, preferences, or other emotional responses? Do you want to measure the number of correct responses to questions or to the time it takes users to complete a task? Will you ask the users themselves what they prefer? Once you know what you want to test, you can plan an effective test in relation to a measurable object.

Once you determine which goals you would like to see accomplished, you can test how effectively you've met these needs during the usability testing phase of the documentation process. Usability goals stress the importance of making your document as usable as possible under the conditions that you identify in the audience, environment, and task analysis. Usability goals provide the basis for later usability testing. Goals set early need to be tested to judge whether they have been adequately accomplished.

11-STEP RESEARCH PROCESS FOR EFFECTIVE USABILITY TESTING

Conducting successful usability test results from standardizing your research methodology:

1. Define the problem

Professional communication research, including feasibility/recommendation reports, usability testing, and technical white papers, is the result of attempting to solve a problem or answer a need. As Charles Kettering, the American inventor, engineer, and holder of 186 patents, once said, "A problem well defined is a problem half solved." The process of defining a problem begins by listing possible causes of the symptoms.

2. Establish research objectives

What information do you need to solve the problem? How will you gather this information? What research instrument will you use? The answers to these questions will ensure you progress toward meaningful research.

3. Review secondary (existing) research and determine if primary (new) research is still needed

Do case studies and technical white papers exist that can solve the problem or guide you toward solving it?

4. Determine what type of primary research will best suit your needs

Should you conduct an online survey, distribute a questionnaire, or have a one-on-one or telephone interview?

Qualitative and Quantitative Information

Quantitative and qualitative research are the two major types of research.

- **Quantitative research** determines and predicts the attitudes, opinions, and behavior of users based on a scientific sampling. Telephone, in-person, and email interviews fall into this category. Each may be appropriate for certain research objectives.
- **Qualitative research,** on the other hand, determines why users feel the way they do about certain issues.

These two types of research capture two types of data:

- **Quantitative measurements** – Data that can be measured by a scale, such as the amount of time to find information and perform tasks, or the number of errors made using the documentation.
- **Qualitative measurements** – Data that cannot be measured by a scale, such as subjective comments and reactions from test subjects.

5. Define your target user.

Selecting participants whose background and abilities are representative of a document's intended end-user is crucial in the evaluation process. You will achieve valid results only if the participants you select are typical end-users, or are matched as closely to the user profiling as possible.

Clearly you cannot produce sound goals and objectives until you understand the users, the environment in which users must work, and the tasks that they want to perform. Your users care more about their work than your product. They want you to organize the major part of your technical writing around the tasks they see in front of them, to tell them how to use your product to do their work.

You can create a user profile by asking the following questions.

TABLE 7.1

What is the purpose of your audience using your document?	Once you have determined what the purpose is, you can make some general assumptions about the user's needs, based on the typical characteristics of that audience type. Your technical document should provide information that specifically addresses this purpose.

TABLE 7.1 (continued)

What similar type of technical information might the audience be familiar with?	People tend to approach tasks in ways that are already familiar to them. Users will appreciate a consistent design and approach.
What is the educational level of the audience?	The answer to these questions provides insight into your audience's reading level. The language, sentence lengths, and style you use will differ depending on this answer. Remember that highly sophisticated and educated specialists in one field often lack the skills, vocabulary, and interest in another field (such as computer technology).
What is the audience's experience?	You need to know how experienced the users are with computers. A user may be an expert in a particular subject but be a novice computer user. To address such a user, your page must present the computer instructions at a fairly basic level.
What is the audience's work environment like?	Or will they have enough peace and quiet to really study the documentation and read it in depth? The document's design and level of detail must match the audience's ability to concentrate on the information presented.
What is the audience's interest level?	Some audiences may be interested in the product to a point, but they are busy people. They will be in no mood to read extensive prose material—they want to get straight to the information. Other audiences may prefer to read contextual explanations. Still other audiences may be computer-phobic or genuinely hostile to a product. Your organization, tone, and format will change depending upon the user's interest in what you write.

6. Create a testing plan

You should create a testing plan before designing the questionnaire or survey. This document should state the research purpose and objectives, define the participant profile, outline the timeline, establish the environment in which the testing will be conducted, and outline the reporting content.

7. Design your questionnaire or survey

Designing the questionnaire or survey is critical step in capturing useful data. You should design for simplicity and brevity when creating usability testing questionnaires. Minimize complicated instructions. Minimize responses that require extensive writing, such as open-ended questions. Instead, use check-boxes, scales, true–false statements, and short fill-ins. Close-ended questions eliminate any advantage users with good writing skills may have over those with poor writing skills.

TABLE 7.2

TYPES OF QUESTIONS

Likert scales	Scales on which participants register their agreement or disagreement with a statement. (The example below is based on a five-point scale.) Overall I found this document easy to use. (Check one) ___Disagree ___Strongly disagree ___Agree ___Strongly agree ___Neither agree nor disagree
Semantic differentials	Semantic differentials are scales on which participants are asked to register the degree to which they favor one of two adjective pairs. Using a rating scale, the participant would circle the number nearest the term that most closely matches his or her feelings about the product. Contemporary 2 1 0 1 2 Traditional Simple 2 1 0 1 2 Complicated Expensive 2 1 0 1 2 Inexpensive Familiar 2 1 0 1 2 Unfamiliar
Fill-in questions	These types of questions provide more latitude for the participants since they are free to say whatever they like, rather than choosing from a predetermined list. Usually you will limit the room with the provision that they may expand their answers in the interview session. I found the following aspects of the documentation easy to use. (List up to three.) ____________________ ____________________ ____________________
Check-box questions	These questions allow the participants to choose from a pre-selected list of options. Please check the statement that most closely approximates your feelings about the navigation. ___I was able to find what I was looking for with no difficulty. ___I found the navigation difficult to use.
Nominal-Scaled Questions	Provide only descriptions such as male/female, designer/developer, or web design shop/government agency/educational institution.
Ordinal-Scaled Questions	Provide description and order, but do not indicate how far apart the descriptors are on the scale. Response selections such as beginner/intermediate/advanced or once per week/once per month/once per quarter/once every six months are examples.

TABLE 7.2 (continued)

Interval-Scaled Questions	Use descriptors that are equal distance apart. Response selections such as strongly agree–strongly disagree or completely satisfied–completely dissatisfied are examples. In these examples you impose a belief that equal intervals exist between the descriptors. You would probably assume that each designation was one unit away from the preceding one.
Ratio-Scaled Questions	Interval-scaled questions with a true zero point. Response selections such as $0, $50, $100, $150, $200 or 0, 5, 10, 15, 20, 25, 30 are examples.

8. Pretest your questionnaire or survey against a subset of your sample users

Depending upon your test design, you may want the participants to fill out the questionnaire either during or immediately after following the testing session, or at both times. Ask preference-related questions that deal with that which you cannot directly observe, such as feelings, opinions, and suggestions for improvement. Do not ask performance-related questions that can be more accurately answered through direct observation.

You should make the pretest as real as possible. You should learn the following:

- How long did the questionnaire or survey take?
- Were there any questions for which you could not find an answer?
- Were there any questions in which you found more than one answer and had difficulty deciding which one to pick?
- Did you need more information to provide only one answer to any of the questions?
- Were there any questions which annoyed you?
- At what point did you want to stop?

You can find the answers to these questions by having the pre-tester take the test once and time it. Then on a second pass through the questionnaire walk through each question and ask the pre-tester probing questions for each of the selections. Does he or she understand the definition of each selection? An alternative method is to ask the pre-tester to talk through the survey as he/she is taking it.

9. Edit and revise the questionnaire or survey

Like other forms of technical communication, this type of research is iterative. You should go through a necessary drafting process. Rarely will you create a questionnaire or survey that does not need fine-tuning.

10. Collect and analyze data

Keep printouts of screen shots on hand during and after usability testing. Then after each test, take a highlighter and highlight any areas where you observe a problem and jot down any quick notes about what you observe. This method allows you to identify all major usability issues you observe. The next step in your analysis is to identify repeat offenders by examining your highlighter-marked printouts. Look at the success rates and task times and identity those tasks that produced frequent errors. Review your notes and focus on controls, elements, labels, and content that users need to notice, manipulate, or modify in order to achieve their goals. Next, begin looking at connections between errors and the design. You should be able to track down the problems.

11. Prepare and present the final research

At the very least you should include the following in your presentation of the final research report:

A. Objectives
B. Methodology – population definition, sample plan, sample size, response rate, limitations, and assumptions
C. Results
D. Conclusions and Recommendations
E. Appendices of supporting documentation

PORTFOLIO BUILDER 7.1 – USABILITY TEST

1. Create a questionnaire or survey using SurveyMonkey or Google Docs with questions that capture both quantitative and qualitative data.
2. Write a very specific task description for participants to perform.
3. Have the other members of the class participate in testing a set of instructions you have written by first using the document and then completing the survey or questionnaire.
4. Write a memorandum (3–4 pages) that presents a brief user profile of each participant, summarizes the results of these tests, assesses the overall effectiveness of the document, and (most importantly) explains how you will edit the document based upon your findings.

OTHER FORMS OF RESEARCH IN TECHNICAL COMMUNICATION

In addition to usability testing, professional communicators have other forms of research, including focus groups, case studies, and technical white papers.

CASE STUDIES

A case study refers to the collection and presentation of detailed information about a particular participant or small group, frequently including the accounts from the subjects themselves. Case studies are a form of qualitative empirical research that investigates an issue, problem, or technology in a real-world context. Case studies typically use one or two examples to illustrate an issue or what a situation is. One goal of a case study is to offer new variables and questions for further research. Another type of case study that is common in industry white papers is to show how a company's product or service is able to satisfy a customer's need or answer a customer's problem.

FOCUS GROUPS

A focus group is a group discussion among four to twelve individuals, typically lasting an hour and a half to two hours. Focus groups are designed to uncover the reasoning behind customer behavior through a candid discussion of opinions, attitudes, and perceptions. Well designed and conducted focus groups can generate a wealth of information

Typically focus groups are conducted in facilities equipped with a one-way mirror, or video equipment, allowing for direct observation of the group. You then have the opportunity to send in questions on the spot, as the discussion progresses. In addition, you gain better insight into issues by directly observing nonverbal behavior such as nodding heads or facial expressions.

WHITE PAPERS

A white paper is an authoritative report or guide that informs readers concisely about a complex issue and presents the issuing body's philosophy on the matter. It is meant to help readers understand an issue, solve a problem, or make a decision.

Theoretical Foundations

White papers can serve a valuable purpose in presenting theories and methods in technical communication, both for instruction and for research. In this way, we can develop a deeper connection between theory and practice. The exploration of diverse theories of composing, of technology, and of teaching and learning has long been fundamental to the rhetoric. White papers provide a medium for documenting and sharing this exploration.

Technology Sector White Papers

A white paper in the technology sector typically provides an overview of a technology, product, or issue, as well as gives companies a standard format with which to promote their products and ideas. A white paper is a printed or online document that describes a product or technology, how it is used, the benefits that accrue to the buyers, and the overall impact of the technology or product on an organization.

Industry White Papers

In industry, a white paper typically includes an overview of a technology, product, or issue. White papers provide companies and industry organizations a means to promote their products and ideas and industry white papers may take the form of a recommendation report with the company's product(s) being the solution(s) to the problem(s).

For example, a white paper about a product might be organized to answer the following questions that a potential consumer may have:

- What is the customer's problem?
- What technologies have been tried to solve the problem?
- Which technology solves the problem best, and why is it the best choice?
- How is the company qualified to implement this technology?
- Which of the company's products uses the technology, and thus solves the customer's problem?
- How does this product work and how is it applicable to this particular problem?

Guidelines for Writing Industry White Papers

The questions that an industry white paper typically answers are similar to a recommendation report:

- What is the problem?
- What kinds of solutions are available?
- Which solution is best, and why?
- How does the company's product(s) provide the best solution to the problem?

White Paper Specifications

TABLE 7.3

Style	White papers typically do not use jargon or technical language and attempt to be readable to a multi-disciplinary audience, thereby encouraging collaboration among readers of different backgrounds.
Design	White papers, unlike books, are scanned or read quickly for content. Visual queuing, filtering, and paragraph summaries facilitate skimming and scanning.
Advance Organizers	Overviews, introductions, and summaries build upon prior knowledge and organize the readers' thoughts before being introduced to details.
Formatting	Most white papers, both academic and professional, are distributed and read electronically.
Visuals	Graphics are effective when they help audiences interpret and understand the written text. Most white papers have illustrations, but as is the case with other forms of professional communication, visuals in white papers should supplement, clarify, or elucidate—not replace—text. Because many white papers are published online and thus read on-screen, it is important that the visuals are appealing to online readers.
Research	The white paper should provide evidence that you cite credible, objective authorities on the subject. Providing evidence such as this affords you with credibility. References, therefore, are important to an effective white paper in establishing and maintaining credibility.
Examples	You may consider using case studies and examples in addition to theoretical concepts and models. Case studies and real-world examples deepen the reader's understanding and make the white paper more appealing and persuasive.
Dissemination	Most white papers are downloadable from the web as PDFs. HTML is less often used because it gives you less control over the layout.

PORTFOLIO BUILDER 7.2 – WHITE PAPER

Write a white paper for an industry audience. You have complete freedom in choosing the topic: a theory, technology, practice, pedagogy, or specific computer application. This paper should be 7–10 pages and include a title page which should include your name, department, institution, institutional address, and date of transmittal, as well as an abstract. Additionally, include parenthetical references and a bibliography (if appropriate) and a hyperlinked table of contents.

The end product should be a document suitable for posting as a link off of a company website. Because a white paper is a genre that you may be asked to write in your professional careers, your white paper should include a portfolio entry card.

CHAPTER EIGHT

Technical Reports

Technical reports include lab reports, handbooks, manuals, job descriptions, feasibility and recommendation reports, funding proposals, and workbooks that contain at least 10 pages of body text.

ELEMENTS

A typical technical report consists of the following elements and sections in this order:

TABLE 8.1

Transmittal Correspondence	When you submit documents, particularly those in book format, you accompany them with a letter or memo of transmittal. If your technical report fulfills the requirements of a technical writing course, you would address your letter of transmittal to your instructor. If you were submitting the document to more than one person, you would write a different letter to each individual. Your transmittal correspondence is not bound, nor does it count toward the page numbering in the document. Although the exact content of this type of correspondence depends upon your purpose and situation, a typical one contains the following elements.

SECTION	SHOULD INCLUDE
Introduction	In the introduction, you mention the accompanying document and explain or remind the reader of its topic.
Body	In the body, you describe the audience, purpose, or special features of the document.
Closing	You should end with a short paragraph that states your willingness to work further with the reader or to answer any questions the reader may have. In addition, you should provide your contact information.

TABLE 8.1 (continued)

	Enclosure	Finally, you should include an enclosure line and the title of the document. Documents of 10 or more pages with report elements such as a title page, table of contents, list of illustrations, and an index are stand-alone publications, and thus you should italicize their titles.
Front Cover	Should have color and visuals.	
Back Cover	For elements such as visuals, company addresses, URLs, and/or logos.	
Front Matter	Number all front matter with small Roman numerals.	
Title Page	May include visuals. If duplex printed (two-sided), typically the back of the title page includes copyright information, publication data, and the ISBN. May serve as a cover and title page in PDFs. Counted, but not numbered on the page.	
Table of Contents	Numbered with small Roman numerals. Headings can be numbered or unnumbered, depending upon the style of the document. A technical report should have a table of contents if it has more than one chapter or 10 or more pages in length. It is numbered with small Roman numerals, and it is the first element in front matter that has the page numbers appearing on the page. Should include two or more levels of detail. **1982–1984: Laying the Foundation 15** The Early Years 17 Creating Adobe Systems 23 Steve Jobs and the LaserWriter 33	
List of Illustrations	May be a list of illustrations, list of figures, or a list of tables, depending upon the style. Lists of illustrations are optional, but recommended if the technical report has more than one numbered illustration and more than one chapter. These appear in the table of contents and are numbered with small Roman numerals. Should include numbers and labels. Table I. Time Schedule 7	
Abstracts & Executive Summaries	The abstract and executive summary are key components to reports because they allow readers to quickly decide whether or not they need or want to read the entire document. What they both share is their specific role in the document, their content, and their structure: • These summaries are both stand-alone documents, meaning that you should think of them as being independent from the report. The readers of the summary may not read the entire report. • Correspondingly, readers of the entire report may not have read the abstract or summary. • These documents are entirely a summary of the report. Do not add any information that is not in the report.	

TABLE 8.1 (continued)

	Components These summaries should contain all key elements of the report. Given the structure of engineering research papers, this includes the following information: • **Situation** – Provide contextualizing information. • **Problem(s)** ° Define the problem(s) that the paper addresses. • **Solution** – Describe the solution: its key characteristics, fundamental principles, and how it solves the problem. • **Evaluation** – Evaluate how well the solution solves problem. • **Recommendations** – Give suggestions for future work or implementation.
Executive Summary	All feasibility/recommendation reports and proposals should have an executive summary. An executive summary details the purpose and scope of the document as well as its conclusions and recommendations.
Preface	Typically describes the purpose and scope of the manual and includes an overview of the parts of the manual. **Preface contents** The preface may contain all or some of the following sections: • The purpose of the manual in one or two sentences • Who should read the manual • The level of technical sophistication or knowledge the reader must possess to use the manual effectively • How the manual is organized • Related manuals • Typographic conventions used in the manual (special characters, symbols, or typography)
Body	Restart the page count using Arabic numbers (1, 2, 3) within the body of the report. Each chapter or section should have a corresponding fly (sectional title) page.
Fly Pages	Like a title page, fly pages count toward the page count, but the pagination does not appear on the page. Each first-level in the table of contents should have a corresponding fly page. For instance, in the following example, "1982–1984: Laying the Foundation" should be a fly page on page 15 of the document. **1982–1984: Laying the Foundation 15** The Early Years 17 Creating Adobe Systems 23 Steve Jobs and the LaserWriter 33

TABLE 8.1 (continued)

	Similar to a title page, a fly page may include visuals, but it can also have any or all of the following: • Learning objectives • A sectional table of contents • An advance organizer that summarizes the chapter or section
Body-Text	Numbered with Arabic numbers.
End Matter	End matter consists of material outside the main body of the document. End matter is supplemental material such as appendixes, glossaries, reference pages, and indexes. All end matter is numbered by continuing the numbering of the body text.
Glossary or List of Symbols	A glossary is an alphabetical list of terms, phrases, abbreviations, and acronyms that may not be clear to the reader. Technical writers often consult subject-matter experts about definitions. As a rule of thumb, a glossary should be approximately 2% the total number of pages in the document. Typically, you place a glossary before an appendix at the end of a document. The reader is instructed in the introduction or a footnote to find highlighted text in the glossary. You may place one in the introduction of a document if there are only a few words, all of which are essential to understanding the document. **Terms to include in glossaries** • Key terms that will be new to the users or are used in a new way • Acronyms and abbreviations • Technical terms, including verbs and phrases used in special ways in the document
Appendix	Appendixes include materials that are not essential parts of your main text but that will provide useful reference information to readers seeking more detail. Some typical materials included in an appendix are detailed explanations and elaborations too technical for the main text, additional diagrams, additional tables summarizing data, technical specifications, and long lists and tables. Appendixes are numbered with capital letters: Appendix A, Appendix B, Appendix C, and so on, and an appendix should always have an in-text reference.
Index	All manuals, handbooks, and reports over 10 pages should have an index. **When your report needs an index** A document needs an index if it has 10 or more pages. This rule applies to any type of document, from simple user guides to technical reference manuals.

TABLE 8.1 (continued)

	Parts of a document to index Use the main body of the document as the source for most of the index entries. Otherwise, include just the sections that add unique information or are not mentioned elsewhere: • Preface • Tables and figures • Footnotes • Appendixes • Glossaries **Topics to include in an index** To determine whether a topic requires an index entry, analyze the topic for the following attributes. Create an index entry for topics related to: • **How to perform a task** – Tasks are the key subjects in certain types of documents, such as installation manuals • **Definitions of terms** – Definitions are frequently the key to a reader's understanding of the information in a document. Therefore, an index should make it easy for a reader to find the definition. • **Acronyms or abbreviations** – The meanings of acronyms and abbreviations are similar to definitions. • **Warnings** – Awareness of the restriction might help a reader avoid making a costly or annoying mistake. • **Concepts or ideas** – This type of topic is most helpful to a reader; however, creating index entries that describe a concept or an idea is fairly difficult. The difficulty is in trying to describe the whole concept in one or two words. Note: Avoid using headings as index entries. Subheadings (Heading 2s) are more appropriate.
References	Follow the style within to the discipline—APA, MLA, or *Chicago Manual of Style*. May be a house style guide.
Colophon	A colophon is an inscription placed at the end of a book or manuscript usually with facts about its production. In most cases it describes the text typography, including the names of the primary typefaces used and a brief description of the type's history. A colophon may also identify the book's designer, the computer software used, the printing method, the printing company, and the kind of ink, paper, and the paper's cotton content. Detailed colophons are a characteristic feature of limited edition and private press printing.

BINDING

Many forms of assembly fall under the heading of binding, from stitching to book-binding. The most common forms of binding are saddle stitching and perfect binding, in which pages are grouped into a bundle, anchored with an adhesive, and then bound with tape or paper binding to hold them together.

Additional binding methods include coil bind, comb binding, saddle stapling, and velo binding. The binding method may require that you have a specified margin (binding width, which is typically one-fourth of an inch), so that it clears the punching or binding area.

When you have a printed project that's more than one piece of paper, you need to determine the binding, the manner of holding the pages together.

Plastic comb binding	Uses a plastic insert with teeth that fit into rectangular holes in the cover and paper. A binding method in which pages are punched and then a comb-like piece of curved plastic is inserted, usually at the left or top edge. The teeth of the curved comb curl into the punched holes, and the curvature of the insert draws it closed. Comb binding allows the finished document to open flat, which makes it suitable for textbooks and workbooks. Since the exterior of the bound piece is solid, the spine can be imprinted with the title of the document, though this is difficult so infrequently done. 

Spiral binding	Uses a metal or plastic spiral with coils. Unlike the comb binding, it's almost impossible to add pages to this type of binding. Pages are punched usually at the left or top edge and then a single coil or spiral of plastic or wire is threaded through the punched holes to anchor the pages together. This type of binding is useful for presentations and workbooks because the pages lie flat when the document is opened. It is also suitable for notebooks, cookbooks, and textbooks. One disadvantage is that there is no printable spine. 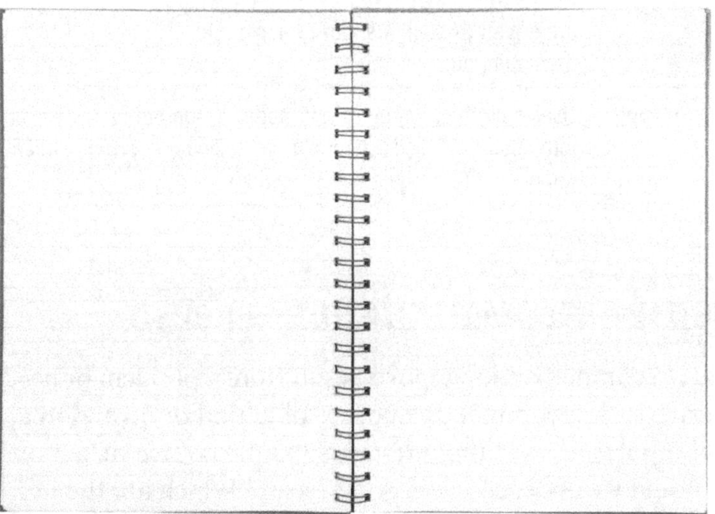
Velo binding	Uses two plastic strips on either side of the document. These strips are held together with plastic pins and bound together with heat. 

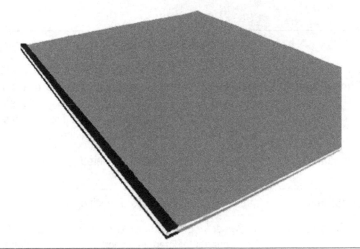

Saddle-stapled binding	Uses two or more staples inserted right at the fold of the paper. The pages of the document need to be printed on both sides (duplex) in the correct position for the final binding. Binding multiple pages together with metal staples. Often used for magazines and catalogs. In saddle stapling, wire is fed from a roll, then cut to form staples, which are driven through a sheaf of paper and then crimped.
Fastback or tape binding	Uses a cloth or paper strip wrapped around the spine of the pages and then glued into position. This is the most professional-appearing binding, but the pages will fall out if the document is used a lot.

FEASIBILITY/RECOMMENDATION REPORTS

Feasibility/recommendation reports result from a problem or need. Then based upon certain criteria, it recommends a course of action or no action at all. These types of technical reports answer the questions "Is the course of action feasible?" "Which option should we choose?" or in some cases "Which are the best options?

Standard Recommendation Report Elements

SECTION	CONTENT/PURPOSE
Introduction	For many feasibility reports, you'll need to discuss the problem, need, or opportunity that has brought about this report.
Technical Background	Some feasibility reports may require some technical discussion in order to make the rest of the report meaningful to readers. Maybe all the technical background can be included in its own section—either toward the front of the report or in an appendix.
Methods of Research	Clearly shows that you have gathered your information through reliable and consistent methods.
Overview of Options	Introduces and fully explicates each option.
Statement of Criteria	Follows order of importance with the most important first. Establishes the standards to determine whether a specific solution is successful and to decide intelligently among the different solutions.
Evaluation of Options	Organized around the different options or around the criteria used to evaluate the options. Graphically represented in tabular format.

Conclusion	Summarizes the evaluation of each option and interprets and synthesizes the information presented in the body according to the purpose of the study.
Recommendations	Has recommendations based on sound research, including primary and secondary sources. States which option can best solve the problem or which option can best meet the needs of the reader.
Appendixes	May contain interviews, surveys, and/or questionnaires.
References	Should have an identifiable, consistent method of documenting sources. Should follow the same page design established in the report.

Sample Recommendation Report

36 Peak Dr.
Building 331, Apt. 1-L Cullowhee, NC 28723
10-25-2014

Dr. Kenneth R. Price
Department of English
Western Carolina University Cullowhee, NC 28723

Subject: English 305 Semester Project

Dear Dr. Price:
Please accept my semester project for ENGL 305 Technical Writing. As you may recall, my project proposal indicated that I was writing a recommendation report on the establishment of a Creative Writing major at Western Carolina University.

While working on this project, I learned that there are a select few universities that offer a Creative Writing program. This information indicates that the creation of a Creative Writing degree at WCU would allow Western's English Department to stand out since it would provide a program scarcely offered at other universities. Additionally, a Creative Writing program could attract a greater number of students interested in enrolling at WCU, because the degree program would establish a diverse writing program and also employ a diverse and talented faculty. My proposal demonstrates the benefits that would accompany the establishment of a Creative Writing degree at Western Carolina University while taking into consideration the cost of its implementation.

Throughout work on this project, I thoroughly researched reliable sources, such as the Board of Governor's guidelines to the establishment of a degree program, as well as other universities' creative writing curriculums.

If you have any questions or would like to discuss my project further, please contact me at sddavis2001@catamount.wcu.edu or (828) 555-2355.

Sincerely,

Stephen D. Davis

Enclosure: *A Recommendation Report: Establishing A Creative Writing Major at Western Carolina University*

RECOMMENDATION REPORT

Establishing A Creative Writing Major at Western Carolina University

Stephen D. Davis

Western Carolina University

November 25, 2018

Contents

Executive Summary

Here at Western Carolina University (WCU), we are fortunate to have a diverse English Department that enables the school to specialize in majors and minors that shape the development of students' writing capabilities. Unfortunately, this talented and well-published faculty of WCU's English Department does not currently offer a major in Creative Writing. For my semester project, I have planned and prepared a curriculum for a major in this field.

Initially, I researched the requirements and standards established by the University of North Carolina Board of Governors regarding the creation and implementation of a Creative Writing Program at WCU. This enabled me to have a better understanding about what is necessary to establish a curriculum that meets university standards. Additionally, I investigated the Creative Writing curriculum of four universities that offer an undergraduate degree in Creative Writing in order to gain a thorough understanding of the types of courses that make up a sufficient program. I have reviewed 12 websites to gather information about job opportunities and other universities' creative writing curriculums in order to be able to create a comprehensive outline for a creative writing program at WCU.

I strongly recommend that WCU establish an undergraduate bachelor degree in Creative Writing because it will allow students to focus on a particular concentration of creative writing (like poetry, fiction, or nonfiction), increase WCU's English graduates' marketability, and establish WCU's English Department of one of the select few who offers a degree program in Creative Writing, which will help bring in a wider writer- oriented student base for the English Department. I recommend that WCU employ two additional lecturers in the English Department to provide classes necessary to establish and maintain a successful Creative Writing program. On average, the employment of two lecturers should cost approximately $100,430. This cost should be offset within the first few years of the program. Once the Creative Writing major is established, students will begin to enroll with the intent to earn a Creative Writing degree, which will compensate for the expense incurred at the program's inception.

Introduction

Many universities do not offer a Creative Writing major. Like WCU, most universities I researched offer only a minor in Creative Writing, ignoring the demand for and benefits of offering a full-fledged major. WCU already has a premier English Department Faculty, many of whom specialize in creative writing, whether it is in fiction, nonfiction, or poetry. In order to make WCU one of the unique universities that offers a Creative Writing degree, I recommend that the English Department expand the Creative Writing minor into a Creative Writing major.

In the report that follows, I will demonstrate how the implementation of a Creative Writing program would benefit WCU. While WCU offers a Creative Writing minor, the expansion of a Creative Writing major would benefit students, faculty, and WCU alike. WCU already offers small and intimate writing-intensive courses that are instrumental in the development of its English graduates, yet a vital aspect of a well-rounded writer is lacking because of the absence of substantial creative writing intensive courses.

With the implementation of a Creative Writing program, WCU would establish a more diverse writing program and also employ a larger talented faculty. Although the expansion of the minor into a major would cost approximately $100,430 for the addition of two faculty lecturers, the rewards would be immense. Students could specialize in a particular area of creative writing, although they would still receive fundamental instruction in critical evaluation and the editing process.

It is my sincere hope that this report will encourage WCU to consider expanding the Creative Writing program and offer a degree in Creative Writing. The expansion of the program would allow students to actively engage with other students who share their interests. Eventually, the skills the program provides will enhance potential Creative Writing majors' marketability, allowing them the opportunity to pursue their dream careers.

DEFINING A LEGITIMATE PROGRAM

Definition of A Degree Program

The University of North Carolina (UNC) Board of Governors "is the policy-making body legally charged with 'the general determination, control, supervision, management, and governance of all affairs of the constituent institutions" (*Board of Governors*, 2008).

The UNC-Board of Governors defines as legitimate degree program as a "program of study in a discipline specialty that leads to a degree in that distinct specialty area at particular level of instruction."

Furthermore, a program of study in a discipline specialty has the following requirements in order to be considered for degree program status:

- A course of study should require at least 27 semester hours in the proposed program area at the undergraduate level.
- Anything less than this within an existing degree program should be designated a concentration, a decision that can be made at the campus level.

WCU similarly defines a degree program or major as one that,

> consists of a group of prescribed and elective courses (totaling at least 27 hours) providing breadth and depth in an academic discipline, in two or more closely related disciplines, or in an interdisciplinary field of study. The requirements for a major in one discipline may include supporting courses selected from other disciplines.
> In degree programs that include a major of 27–45 hours, a minor, second major, or another approved program also is required.
> In degree programs that do not require a minor or second major, 46–64 hours are required in a major, including any concentrations, emphases, or specialization options that may be a part of the major. (*WCU* Catalogue, 2008)

Academic Planning Procedures

> In order to establish new degree programs, one must follow academic planning procedures established by the UNC-Board of Governors. First, one must notify the UNC-Board of Governors of the intent to plan a new baccalaureate degree program.

According to the UNC-Board of Governors,

> It is expected that funding to support new degree programs will be provided through a combination of internal reallocations, enrollment increase funds, and external grants. Where appropriate (i.e., in cases where there is convincing evidence of potential for program success if initial support is provided) and when central funds are available, start-up funds will be provided, generally for no more than three years, with the expectation that the program will ultimately be self-sustaining and the start-up funds will be returned and recycled for the use of other UNC programs. In cases where the allocation of start-up funds is appropriate but they are not immediately available, recommendation of approval of the program may be delayed until such funds are available. (*Academic Planning*, 2008)

One must consider the following aspects of a degree program prior to planning its implementation:

- A brief description of the program and a statement of educational objectives.
- The relationship of the proposed new program to the institutional mission and how the program fits into the institution's strategic plan.

- The relationship of the proposed new program to other existing programs at the institution.
- Special features or conditions that make the institution a desirable, unique, or appropriate place to initiate such a degree program (*Academic Planning*, 2008).

In addition, one must "list all other public and private institutions of higher education in North Carolina currently operating programs similar to the proposed new degree program, estimate the number of students that would be enrolled in the program during the first year of operation, including full-time and part-time students" (*Academic Planning*, 2008).

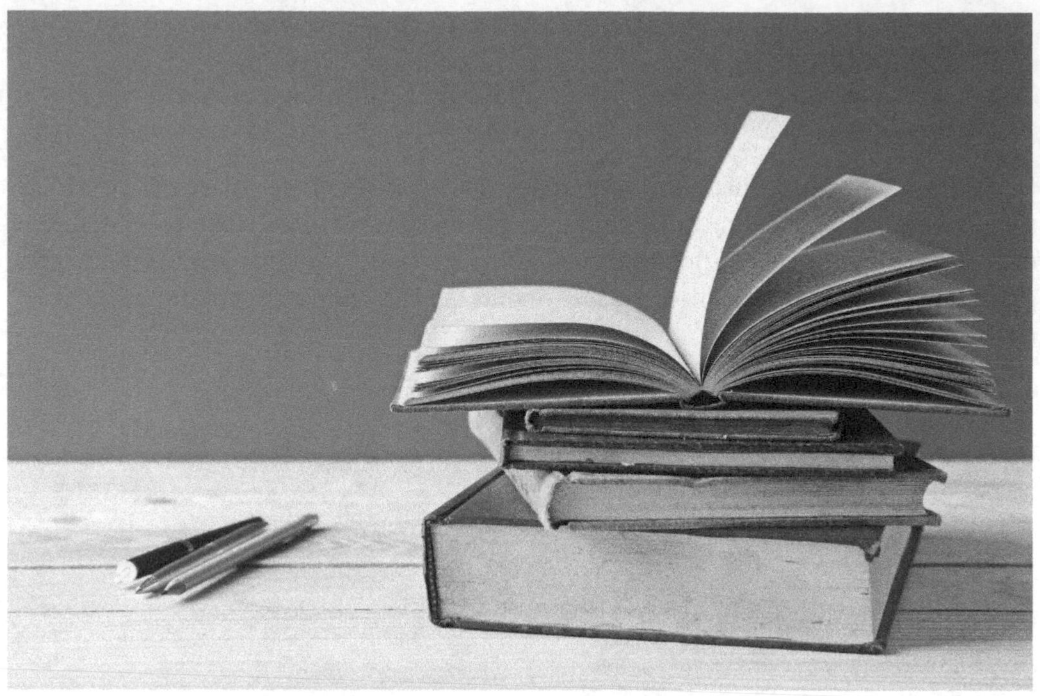

A COMPREHENSIVE CREATIVE WRITINGCURRICULUM

WCU's Existing Creative Writing Minor

WCU currently offers a minor in Creative Writing, although it does not provide a corresponding major. The Creative Writing minor requires 18 hours, including 12 hours selected from the following courses:

- ENGL 303 – Introduction to Professional Writing and Editing
- ENGL 308 – Nonfiction Writing
- ENGL 309 – Poetry Writing
- ENGL 405 – Advanced Creative Writing
- ENGL 493 – Topics in Creative Writing
- ENGL 497 – Senior Seminar in Writing
- MPTP 310 -–Introduction to Screenwriting

The minor also requires 6 hours of literature courses, exclusive of those approved for general education credit (*WCU English Department*, 2008).

Other Universities' Creative Writing Degree Programs
I have collected data regarding three universities that offer a Creative Writing Degree in order to demonstrate the practicality and ease with which WCU's existing Creative Writing Minor can be expanded into a full-fledged degree program.

Carnegie Mellon English Department: BA in Creative Writing
Carnegie Mellon's English Department provides a Creative Writing degree. Creative Writing majors are required to take:

- At least two Survey of Forms (introductory workshop) courses.
- At least four workshops.
- A total of 12–24 hours of writing workshops.
- A total of 6–18 hours of other writing courses.
- A total of 18 or more hours of literature courses (*Curriculum*, 2008).

While WCU's Creative Writing Minor provides only 21 hours of writing courses, Carnegie Mellon's Creative Writing Program provides choices from at least 42 hours of courses. Although WCU's minor requires that only 6 hours of literature courses be taken in order to meet the minimum requirements, the Carnegie Mellon Creative Writing Program requires 18 or more hours of literature courses.

The University of California, Riverside's Creative Writing Program

The University of California, Riverside's Creative Writing Program provides an extensive variety of courses for majors to choose from, which enables students to specialize in the particular area of Creative Writing that interests them. The University of California's Creative Writing Program is structured as follows:

1. Pre-requisite: CRWT 056. Introduction to Creative Writing
2. Lower Division Requirements (20 hours, five courses):
   A. Two Creative Writing survey courses from:

CRWT 046A – Craft of Writing: Survey in Contemporary Fiction CRWT 046B – Craft of Writing: Survey in Contemporary Poetry CRWT 046C – Craft of Writing: Survey in Contemporary Nonfiction

   B. Two Creative Writing introductory courses from: CRWT 057A – Introduction to Fiction

CRWT 057B – Introduction to Poetry
CRWT 057C – Introduction to Creative Nonfiction

   C. One literature survey course.

3. Upper Division Requirements (60 hours):
   A. Three workshop courses in primary genre: Creative Nonfiction, Poetry, or Fiction.
   B. Repeat one advanced workshop in primary genre of interest or other course approved by the department.
   C. One workshop in second genre.
   D. One workshop in third genre.
   E. Three upper-division courses in Creative Writing.
   F. One upper-division course in Art, Art History, Music, Dance, or Theatre.
   G. Four (4) units of CRWT 195 or CRWT 195H (Senior Honors Thesis) or approved course from list available in department.
   H. Four upper-division courses of concentration in another discipline or set of disciplines approved by advisor (*Undergraduate Program*, 2008).

Unlike WCU's Creative Writing Minor, the Creative Writing Program at the University of California, Riverside enables students to participate in many levels of workshops in order to hone their writing capabilities.

The University of Colorado's Creative Writing Option of the English Major

The University of Colorado's Creative Writing Option of the English Major requires stu- dents of the Creative Writing Program to take 39 credit hours (*Creative Writing Option*, 2006). Creative Writing majors must satisfy the following requirements:

I. Option-Specific Requirements (12 hours, four courses)
ENGL 1400 – Intro. to Literary Studies
ENGL 1601 – Telling Tales: Narrative Art in Literature and Film
or ENGL 2250 – Introduction to Film
ENGL 2154 – Introduction to Creative Writing
ENGL 3001 – Critical Writing

II. Advanced Course Work (12 hours, four courses)
Student must complete all courses in poetry or fiction area.

A. Poetry

ENGL 3020 – Poetry Workshop
ENGL 4025 – Advanced Poetry Workshop
ENGL 4080 – History of the English Language, or ENGL 4160 – Poetics
ENGL 4166 – History of American Poetry, or ENGL 4320 – History of Poetry in English

B. Fiction

ENGL 3050 – Fiction Workshop
ENGL 4055 – Advanced Fiction Workshop
ENGL 4200 – History of the English Novel I, or ENGL 4210 – History of English Novel II
ENGL 4230 – The American Novel, or ENGL 4236 – The American Short Story

III. Required Area Electives (12 hours, four courses)

A. Choose three literary courses.
B. Choose one additional workshop course.

IV. Internship or Senior Writing Project (3 credit hours)

The University of Colorado's Creative Writing Program bears a resemblance to WCU's Professional Writing Program, which requires an 18-hour core (including an internship, core English courses, and core writing courses), 12 writing electives, and 6 additional hours of English Literature Courses at the junior or senior level.

The Construction of a Comprehensive Creative Writing Curriculum

Since WCU has an established Creative Writing minor, constructing a comprehensive Creative Writing Curriculum should not be too difficult. If our university increased the number of creative writing courses offered each semester, students would be capable of earning the required courses that a legitimate degree program requires.

WCU could create a Creative Writing concentration based upon a similar structure as the Professional Writing Concentration that it currently provides. This major would require a minimum of 42 hours to a maximum of 60 hours as follows:

- Foreign Language Requirement, 6 hours

MFL 231 and MFL 232

- Core, 18 Hours

Includes survey courses, introductory writing courses, and a writing internship or coop.

- Writing Electives, 12–24 hours in a particular creative writing concentration Poetry, Fiction, or Creative Nonfiction
- Junior/Senior Literature Electives, 6–12 hours

If WCU offers a more comprehensive selection of writing electives, students who pursue a Creative Writing concentration will become knowledgeable in writing for a particular concentration like poetry, fiction, or creative nonfiction. The WCU Creative Writing minor is inadequate because it is limited by the number of courses available for credit.

Unlike other universities' Creative Writing Programs, a comprehensive Creative Writing Curriculum at WCU will incorporate proficiency in a foreign language up to the 231-232 level. Since the major requires only between 42 and 60 hours in the concentration, students will have the opportunity to pursue a minor that will further enhance their educational experience.

Cost of Expanding the Creative Writing Minor

Although budget cuts to the North Carolina University system may negatively impact the development of prospective degree programs like a Creative Writing program, WCU has an advantage in the development process since it already has a Creative Writing minor. Expansion of the Creative Writing minor into a full-fledged program could be cost efficient for the university. Table I shows the average salary faculty received in throughout the United States in 2007–2008.

TABLE I: Average Faculty Salary, 2007–2008 (*Inside Higher Ed*, 2008)

CATEGORY	AVERAGE SALARY
Full Professor	$103,521
Associate Professor	$73,275
Assistant Professor	$61,359
Instructor	$44,382
Lecturer	$50,215
Unranked Full-Time	$56,811

The majority of universities that do offer a Creative Writing program have an average of eight faculty members devoted to the program. According to the Spring 2009 registrar, WCU currently employs six writing faculty:

- Pamela Duncan, Assistant Professor
- Deidre Elliot, Assistant Professor
- Karen Greenstone, Lecturer
- Deepak Pant, Lecturer
- Kenneth Price, Assistant Professor
- Ron Rash, Parris Distinguished Professor in Appalachian Cultural Studies

The majority of these professors are assistant professors or lecturers. According to the data from table I, the average assistant professor's salary is $61,359, while the average lecturer's salary is $50,215. WCU could expand the Creative Writing minor into a full degree with the addition of two lecturers for approximately $100,430. This cost should eventually be offset if the program flourishes and encourages writing students to enroll at WCU within the next few years.

Opportunities and Benefits of a Creative Writing Program

Job Opportunities

A Creative Writing degree, like other English degrees, opens up the path to a multitude of job opportunities and career possibilities.

Possible Career Options

Although an English Degree with a concentration in Creative Writing will enable students to be focused in a particular concentration of creative writing (poetry, fiction, or nonfiction), the courses students will take can enhance their marketability. Because of an increase in writing workshops and other writing courses, Creative Writing majors will have proficient writing and communications skills that are useful in a variety of jobs. Table II lists a variety of career options available to a creative writing major:

TABLE II: Possible Career Options (*Ashland University Career Development Center*, 2008)

Abstract Writer	Advertising Copy Editor
Advertising Executive	Arts Administrator

Bibliographer	Copy Editor
Corporate Communications Critic	Customer Service Representative
Editor	English/Literature Professor
Feature Writer	Grant Writer
Journalist	Lexicographer
Librarian	Literary Agent
Lobbyist	Manuscript Reader
Market Research Analyst	Media Planner
Newspaper/Magazine Journalist	Office Manager
Poet	Policy & Procedure Analyst
Political Campaign Organizer	Proofreader
Public Affairs Coordinator	Public Relations Specialist
Writing Center Director	Publisher
Reporter	Researcher
Screen/Television Script Writer	Senior Editor
Song Writer Specialist	Speech Writer
Technical Writer	Writer/Author

Like Professional Writing majors, Creative Writing majors will have ample job opportunities available to them because they will be highly trained in written communication and research. However, a Creative Writing major would further specialize and enhance the creative facilities and skills of writers, allowing them to remain marketable to mainstream job opportunities while allowing them the ability to pursue creative projects.

Useful Skills Honed by Creative Writing Majors

Like other WCU English majors, Creative Writing majors will develop their technical and creative writing capabilities thoroughly. According to WCU's Career Services, students with English degrees like creative writing should graduate possessing the following skills:

- Ability to write well, speak well, and read carefully
- Research and analytical skills
- Ability to craft well-organized arguments
- Familiarity with computers, including Word Processing, Databases, Presentation Software, and Research tools

- Possession of critical content evaluation skills
- Experience with collaborative projects
- Adept at being detailed oriented (*WCU Careers*, 2008)

Creative Writing majors will also be:

- Highly imaginative
- Proficient in fiction, nonfiction, and poetry writing
- Self-disciplined
- Able to work with deadlines
- Open to criticism
- Individually expressive
- Proficient in editing
- Proficient in critiquing (*University of Wilmington*, 2008)

Each of these skills will allow a Creative Writing major to successfully pursue a variety of opportunities and careers, from editing to writing creative editorials for a magazine like *Sports Illustrated.*

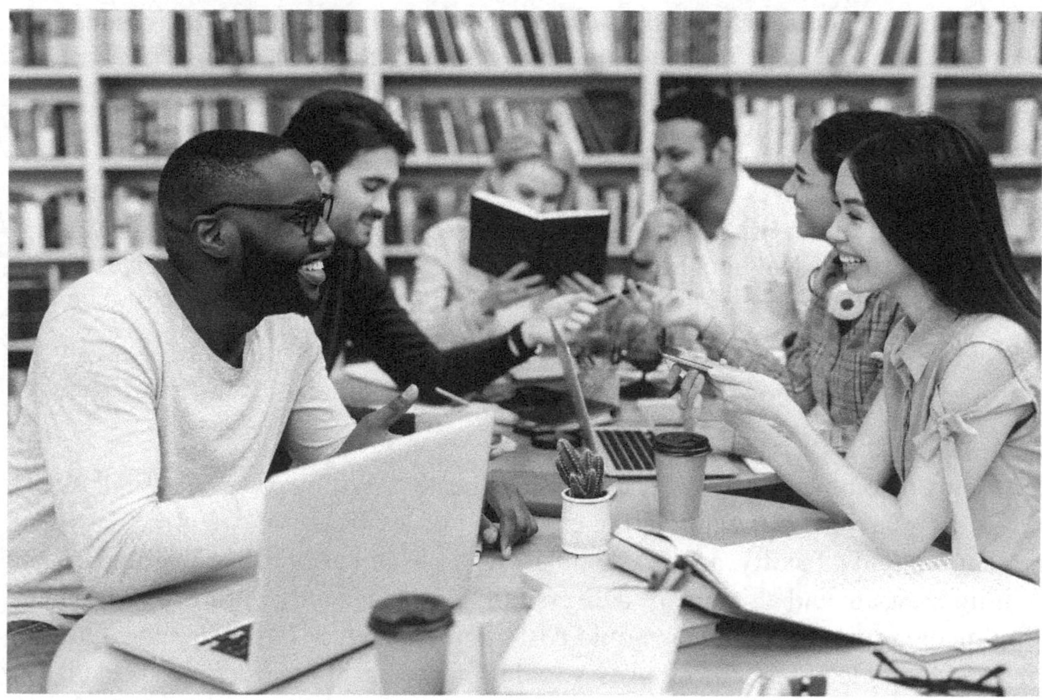

ADVANTAGES OF ESTABLISHING A CREATIVE WRITING DEGREE AT WCU

Advantages of Establishing a Creative Writing Degree at WCU

Ultimately, establishing a Creative Writing degree will:

- **Expand the variety of intensive writing courses offered.** The expansion of a minor in Creative Writing into a major will allow students and faculty to have more choices in the intensive writing courses offered, which will enable students to strengthen their writing capabilities further. Currently, WCU's writing program focuses primarily on professional writing skills, while providing scarce creative writing courses.
- **Challenge students' innovation and imaginative capacities while continuing to hone editing and critical evaluation skills.** Furthermore, establishing a Creative Writing degree would allow students to participate in more courses that suit their writing capabilities and career prospects. Creative Writing majors would be capable of taking courses that challenge their innovation and imaginative capacities while giving them the opportunity to hone their editing and critical evaluation skills through writing work-shops.

- **Provide courses that will enhance students' marketability after graduation.** Because of an increase in writing workshops and other writing courses, Creative Writing majors will have proficient writing and communications skills that are useful in a variety of jobs.
- **Encourage students' who wish to pursue creative writing to enroll at WCU.** Expansion of the minor in Creative Writing into a major will establish a diverse course program for all students pursuing any area of writing, whether it is professional or creative. The availability of more writing intensive courses will make WCU attractive to many students wishing to actively pursue and enhance their writing capabilities.

Recommendation

I strongly recommend that WCU establish a Creative Writing program. While WCU offers a Creative Writing minor, the expansion of a Creative Writing major would benefit students, faculty, and WCU alike. WCU would establish a more thorough writing program and also employ a diverse and talented faculty. Although the expansion of the minor into a major would cost approximately $100,430 for the addition of two faculty lecturers, the rewards would be immense. Students could specialize in a particular area of creative writing, although they would still receive fundamental instruction in critical evaluation and the editing process. The expansion of the program would allow students to actively engage with other students who share their interests. Eventually, the skills that the program provides will enhance potential Creative Writing majors' marketability, allowing them the opportunity to pursue their dream careers.

Text Sources

"Possible Career Options," Ashland University Career Development Center, http://www3.ashland.edu/services/cardev/documents/English_000.pdf

"Curriculum," Carnegie Mellon, 2008, http://english.cmu.edu/degrees/ba_cw/curriculum.html

"Faculty Salaries and Priorities," Inside Higher Ed, 2008, http://www.insidehighered.com/news/2008/04/14/aaup

"The Undergraduate Program," The University of California, Riverside, 2008, http://www.creativewriting.ucr.edu/undergraduate/index.html

"Creative Writing Option of the English Major," The University of Colorado, Denver, 2006, Retrieved from http://thunder1.cudenver.edu/clas/english/majorOptionCreativeWrtg.html

"Board of Governors," The University of North Carolina, 2006, http://www.northcarolina.edu/content.php/system/index.htm

"Academic Planning," The University of North Carolina, 2008, http://www.northcarolina.edu/content.php/aa/planning/index.htm

"Related Major Skills," The University of Wilmington, 2008, http://www.uncwil.edu/stuaff/career/Majors/creativewriting.htm

"Degree Programs and Requirements," Western Carolina University Catalogue, 2008, http://0-catalog.wcu.edu.wncln.wncln.org/content.php?catoid=4&navoid=94

"Bachelor of Arts Degree in English," Western Carolina University Careers, http://careers.wcu.edu/6936.asp

"English Minors," Western Carolina University English Department, http://www.wcu.edu/as/english/pages/minors.html

TRADEMARKS, COPYRIGHTS, & PROPRIETARY INFORMATION

Legal Guidelines

Technical publications professionals need to follow or establish guidelines that cover the protection of intellectual property. Trademarks and materials that can be copyrighted are among a company's most valuable assets. Anyone involved in creating materials that use trademarks or materials subject to copyright has the responsibility to protect a company's copyrights and trademarks.

Sometimes you should check with the legal department in your company. If you do not have a legal department, check with counsel specializing in trademark and copyright law.

COPYRIGHTS

Copyright is a type of legal protection, granted by federal law for most types of intellectual works, including computer programs. With limited exceptions, no one may copy or reproduce, display, prepare derivative works, or distribute copies to the public by sale, rental, lease, lending, or other transfer of ownership of copyrighted works without permission of the copyright owner.

Because copyrights do not protect the ideas and concepts contained in a work, but only the expression of such ideas and concepts, copyright is not always the best means of protecting intellectual property. Confidential business information is usually best protected as a trade secret and should include a proprietary information label.

What You Should Copyright

The following types of materials intended for external distribution should contain a copyright notice:

- Technical publications, including both print and electronic manuals, books, articles, research papers, and brochures
- Advertising copy
- Catalogs
- Product documentation
- Software applications, including source and object code

Check with a legal department if you don't know whether you should copyright a particular type of work.

Copyrighting Your Work

What comprises a copyright notice?

- The symbol © or the word "Copyright"
- The year of first publication of the work
- The name of the owner of the copyright

Your technical publications style guide may have approved specific copyright statements. You should not modify the copyright portion of these statements (except for the date) without first consulting your legal department.

Example of a copyright statement:

> © 2018 Serenity, Inc., 2550 Philbin Avenue, Gilroy, California 95021 U.S.A. All rights reserved. This product and related documentation are protected by copyright and are distributed under licenses restricting their use, copying, distribution, and decompilation. No part of this product or related documentation may be reproduced in any form by any means without prior written authorization of Serenity, Inc., and its licensors, if any.

Duration of Copyright Protection

Copyrights exist for a finite number of years, generally the life of the author plus 50 years or if work made for hire, for 75 years from the date of publication, after which time the work becomes part of the public domain.

Copyright Ownership

Generally speaking, if materials are written by an employee in the course of his or her job, the employer is the owner of the copyright. Copyrights in works created by independent contractors are owned by the independent contractors. However, this ownership is usually transferred to the employer if the contractor has signed a standard Personal Services Agreement.

Registering Your Copyright

To take full advantage of the legal protection afforded a copyrighted work, you may also have to register the work with the United States Copyright Office. Registration requires completing a one-page application and including either a copy of the work or a portion of the source code, usually the first and last 25 pages with portions blocked out to protect trade secret information.

TRADEMARKS

A trademark is a sign, design, or expression that identifies products or services of a particular source from others. Trademarks used to identify services are usually called service marks.

- A **trademark** is a word, phrase, name, symbol, or logo—or a combination of these elements—adopted and used by a company to identify its particular brand of products and services, and to distinguish them from those of other companies.
- A **service mark** is the same as a trademark except that it identifies the source of a service rather than a product.

Types of Trademarks

Trademarks fall into two categories:

- **Registered** – Trademarks registered with the U.S. Patent and Trademark Office or the trademark offices of other countries.
- **Unregistered** – Trademarks claimed by a company but have not been registered.

While both types of trademarks are protectable, registered trademarks are subject to stronger enforcement measures and may be necessary in some countries to prevent others from pirating a company's trademarks.

Proper Use of Trademarks

A company's exclusive rights to its trademarks may be weakened if not used properly, even if they are registered. All company trademarks should have the following:

- The appropriate notice (® or ™) the first time the trademark is mentioned in the text.

- The appropriate legend on the back of the title page attributing the trademarks to a company.

To protect trademarks:

- Use ® with registered trademarks. Don't use this mark with unregistered trademarks or when a registration certificate has not yet been received.
- For unregistered trademarks, use only the ™ designation.

Designate trademarks on book covers and the first time they are mentioned in text, including prefaces, chapters or sections, and appendixes. Most publications do not put trademark symbols in the table of contents, chapter or appendix titles, section heads, tables, or captions.

PROPRIETARY INFORMATION

Proprietary information is any information that gives a company a competitive advantage or any information that can damage a company if disclosed outside of a company's control.

Proprietary information includes the following:

- Detailed information about new products before public announcement
- Drafts of manuals, research papers, and product notes
- Product features and technical data
- Object and source code
- Flowcharts and schematics
- Target dates for production
- Market placement and strategies, pricing, and customer information
- Costs and other financial information
- Design, diagnostic, and reliability data
- Email messages
- Presentation materials (including handouts, transparencies, and slides)
- Employee information, such as performance reviews and salary information

Protecting Proprietary Documents

You should to protect proprietary information by properly labeling it from the time it is created until it is released or safely destroyed.

Three commonly used proprietary labels include the following:

- **Company Name Proprietary: Internal Use Only** – Use this label for general internal information distributed throughout a company.

- **Company Name Proprietary/Confidential: Need-to-Know** – Use this label for all prerelease product documentation and information. This includes all information distributed to product teams, such as engineering specifications, manuals, release notes, and white papers. Most documentation should have this label.
- **Company Name Proprietary/Confidential: Registered** – Use this label for highly sensitive information, where numbered copies are made and carefully controlled.

Protecting Electronic Communication

Technical writers should be just as careful in protecting proprietary information in email messages as they are with any other documents. Label email containing proprietary information in the email header or footer:

- Company Name Proprietary: Internal Use Only
- Company Name Proprietary/Confidential: Need-to-Know

Double-check the names in a company email distribution list before sending information to a large audience, and don't distribute messages beyond the distribution list or to addresses outside of your company.

CREDITS

CHAPTER NINE

Portfolios

As technical communication has moved from traditional print to digital publishing platforms, the need has arisen to redefine the professional portfolio to present this newest medium. The past methodologies of presenting the theoretical and practical education of technical communicators do not apply to the genre of computer documentation in particular.

As evidenced by the increasing number of technical communication positions advertised solely to individuals with online proficiency, writing professionals need new methods of presenting their skills to industry. The area of online documentation has moved technical communication beyond existing research: the types of documents that scholars once suggested should be represented in professional portfolios have moved from memoranda, letters, and step-by-step instructions, to technical proposals, annual reports, policies and procedures manuals, and computer hardware brochures. Research, however, has stopped short of addressing the newer forms of writing common to the computer sector of industry.

WHAT IS A PORTFOLIO?

A portfolio is a collection, typically five or six substantial samples, of materials you have created. Portfolios communicate accomplishments, works in progress, and personal history. Writers and editors use portfolios to showcase their work when applying for a job. A portfolio is essential if you are seeking employment as a technical communicator, for it provides the opportunity to showcase your talents and to tell potential colleagues about yourself.

Why Compile a Professional Portfolio?

Besides the more obvious reason of showing your level of skill in technical communication, your portfolio aids in controlling the direction, pace, and content of job interviews. Perhaps most important is so you can answer "Yes" when a potential employer asks if you have writing samples. And you should assume they will ask.

The move away from the medium of paper to an electronic medium

Traditionally a portfolio was a large book or leather case containing writing, editing, and design samples. Electronic documents should be displayed in the medium for which they were created. Online help systems, web pages, Flash movies, wizards, and instructional movies lose their effectiveness when printed and presented in hard-copy format. Documentation created for online delivery should be delivered in an online form.

Online documentation is dynamic, nonlinear, and interactive, yet all three of these elements are lost when an online document is printed out and presented in a hardcopy portfolio. Online portfolios retain the unique qualities of online documents as well as demonstrate your ability for creating computer documentation.

Why Compile a Digital Professional Portfolio?

The most persuasive portfolio entries are those that demonstrate knowledge. Whereas paper documents may indicate a proficiency with that medium, they do not demonstrate grounding, theoretical or otherwise, in the writing and skills required in the computer industry: online documentation and digital publishing.

The answer to demonstrating online proficiencies is the digital portfolio, a collection of writing samples delivered in an electronic format: CD, DVD, or web page. With digital portfolios, you can share print, design, and interactive work in a variety of ways: email, print, and online.

COLLECTING MATERIALS AND COMPILING YOUR PORTFOLIO

A good portfolio is diverse and demonstrates a wide range of professional writing skills and proficiencies. Determine which of your skills are the ones you want to use in the future. Match those skills and proficiencies to job descriptions and postings. You may want to look for similar jobs at other companies to create a composite list of skills. Use this list to create one portfolio entry for each skill area. If the entry fits in more than one area, make a note of this and provide cross-reference links in both places.

ORGANIZING YOUR PORTFOLIO

The best portfolios are those created from a personalized set of categories and suited to particular positions.

Chronological portfolio

In this type of portfolio, the most recent information is considered the most important. Like a chronological resume, your experience and education is listed in reverse chronological order, with the most recent first.

Functional portfolio

This type of portfolio highlights your qualifications without emphasizing the specific work dates or work history. Rather, this type of portfolio emphasizes professional growth and accomplishments that are related directly to the position for which you are applying. Like a functional resume, this type of portfolio is effective if your skills and abilities come from different professional experiences and times of employment or if you are new to a field or a recent graduate.

Topical Portfolio

This type of portfolio is organized by categories based on your skills and experience. This is the most common and probably the type you will want to create.

CREATING A TOPICAL PORTFOLIO

Creating Grouping Schemes (Filters)

You should group related materials into categories. You have a number of filters or grouping schemes to organize entries in your portfolio:

- **Genre** – Persuasive, instructional, informational, descriptive
- **Technology** – Print, interactive, video, audio
- **Medium** – Print, web, electronic
- **Thematic** – Project type or design principles
- **Client Industry/market** – Computer documentation, public relations, copy writing, product support, editing

Outlining Your Portfolio

To put your entries into outline form, first decide upon the main (first-level) categories. Then decide where each entry fits within these categories. Perhaps you have more than one quick reference cards and only one help system. You can organize them by them a Reference and Support group.

Creating a Site Map

A site map imposes a hierarchy on your portfolio and shows three bits of information at a glance:

- **Grouping** – The grouping scheme you've chosen.
- **Hierarchy** – Where each page or screen fits within the whole of the portfolio.
- **Connections** – What links to and from each page or screen.

One way to map the information is through a flowchart similar to the one below:

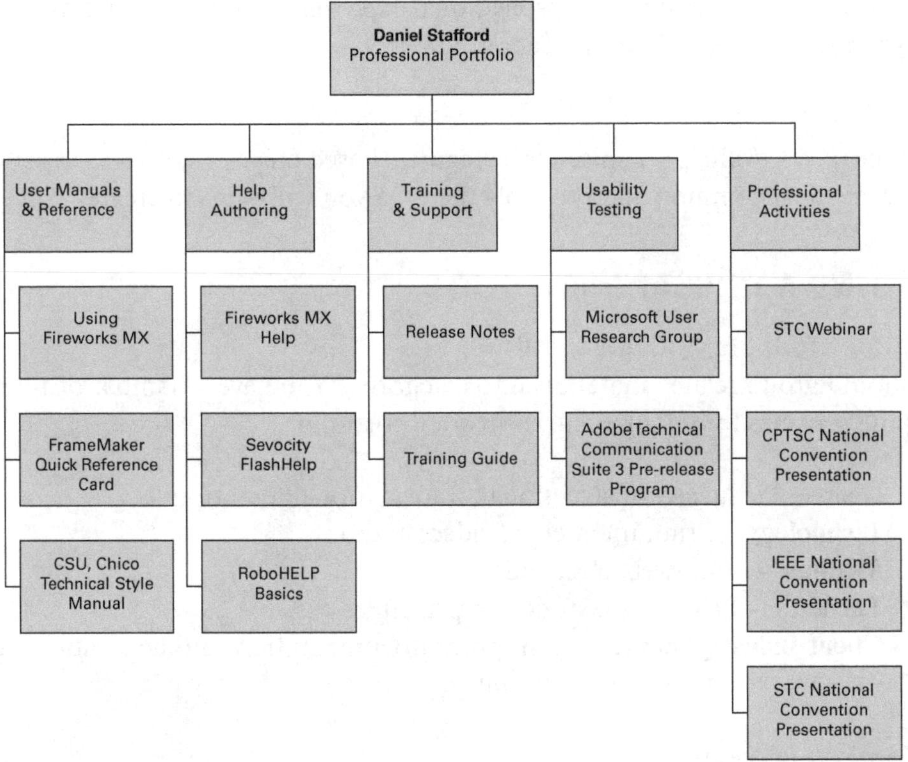

EXERCISE 9.1 – ORGANIZATION

Create an outline, a flowchart, and a site map of your portfolio, including background information:

- Describe, in detail, the position you are seeking—skills, experience, technological proficiencies.
- Create a list of entries in your portfolio.
- Create an outline of main categories to organize your documents into.
- Using the category outline as a guide, draw a flowchart for your portfolio.

PORTFOLIO CONTEXTUALIZING ELEMENTS

An effective portfolio does more than simply tell prospective employers you are qualified for a position. It provides you the opportunity to introduce yourself, to personify the portfolio beyond its entries and a resume.

Prefatory Statements

While a preface typically describes the purpose and scope of the document, a prefatory statement in a portfolio allows you to introduce yourself to your audience, to talk in a personal way about yourself. This statement explains your skill set, training, the projects included in the portfolio, your career interests and goals, and any professional experience. While resumes with photographs have fallen from favor, the advent of social networking sites has created an entire generation of individuals who give no thought to including a photograph or image in their portfolios.

Annotations

Annotations provide a context for the elements and entries in your portfolio. Your portfolio should have narrative introductions to each entry, highlighting your skills, experience, and computer literacies.

- **Annotated tables of contents** present users with an outline and organization of your portfolio. Annotations allow you to describe each entry, as well as accentuate the skills and knowledge you acquired.
- **Annotated entry cards** contextualize each entry into the overall portfolio broader body of work.

These narratives should include specific examples that compare your skills with whatever career area you are interested in.

You should emphasize skills common to the computer industry in your annotations:

TABLE 9.1

SKILLS	ENTRIES
Oral and written communication skills	Conference presentations, white papers, editing mark-ups.
Internationalization/localization	Fluency in a foreign language, translations.
Conflict management	Project management and conflict resolution, such as in a group or team environment.
Creativity and innovation	Developing a variety of different types of documents, using different media.
Teamwork	Experience working on group projects as a member of a group or team.

Project management	Documentation plans and proposals, bringing projects to completion early and/or under budget.
Process and product improvement	Human factors engineering, usability testing and editing.

Annotated tables of contents

In the following example, the entry indicates experience in human factors, usability testing, and computer documentation. This entry would qualify the individual for positions as a technical writer, computer documentation specialist, computer help desk analyst, or usability researcher or analyst.

Annotated entries

Each entry should include a statement that explains the circumstances under which you created it; how the entry represents the range of your writing/editing skills and software proficiencies; the context for the entry; its publication data, including the percentage of work completed; and the software programs you used to create and deliver the entry.

FIGURE 9.2

Kenneth R. Price | Professional Portfolio

Adobe InDesign® Quick Reference Card User Profile/Needs Assessment gives an extended profile of typical users of the quick-reference card, an outline of the key features, and a detailed analysis of how these features typically fit into the user's workflow.	5
Help System Proposal provides an extensive user profile and needs assessment for the documentation, as well as a detailed explanation of how the help system will meet these needs. The proposal includes the usability goals for the documentation and a brief depiction of the individuals who will participate in the technical review.	13
Documentation Plan details the different types of documentation: its target audiences and learning paths; the time schedule; deliverables; resources; individuals involved in usability testing; and the post-project activities.	15
User Manual Layout Grid includes grids of the layouts for different types of pages, as well as a matrix of the different visual elements: format, design, resolution, and placement of graphics, typography and colors, and the types of callouts and screen shots.	23
Usability Testing Questionnaire for iDVD Tutorial provides a questionnaire and survey created with Google Docs to measure the usability attributes of the tutorial.	33

table of contents | resume | electronic mail | contact information

©2011 Kenneth R. Price. All rights reserved.

Depending upon the type of document, entries should include the following information:

- Title
- Role
- Percentage of the work completed
- Keywords
- Description/Abstract
- Release Date
- Running Time
- File Information (format, file size, audio or video)
- Whether the document contains images
- Application(s) used to create it

FIGURE 9.3

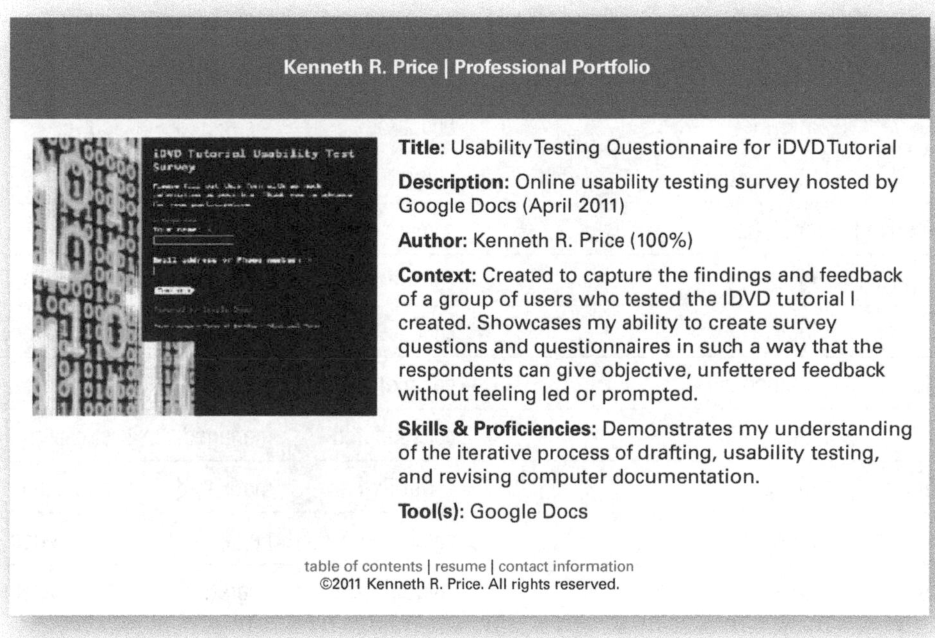

Kenneth R. Price | Professional Portfolio
iDVD Tutorial Usability Test Survey
Title: Usability Testing Questionnaire for iDVD Tutorial
Description: Online usability testing survey hosted by Google Docs (April 2011)
Author: Kenneth R. Price (100%)
Context: Created to capture the findings and feedback of a group of users who tested the IDVD tutorial I created. Showcases my ability to create survey questions and questionnaires in such a way that the respondents can give objective, unfettered feedback without feeling led or prompted.
Skills & Proficiencies: Demonstrates my understanding of the iterative process of drafting, usability testing, and revising computer documentation.
Tool(s): Google Docs
table of contents | resume | contact information
©2011 Kenneth R. Price. All rights reserved.

Action verbs and performance descriptors specific to the computer industry

You should use the same language in your annotations as you do in your resume's experience descriptions.

TABLE 9.2

PERFORMANCE DESCRIPTORS			ACTION VERBS FOR ACCOMPLISHMENT STATEMENTS		
accurate	generous	self-controlled	accomplished	headed	reorganized
active	good-natured	sensible	achieved	helped	researched
aggressive	honest	serious	administered	identified	revised
alert	humorous	significant	advanced	implemented	scheduled
ambitious	imaginative	sincere	analyzed	improved	served
analytical	independent	sociable	approved	increased	set up
artistic	individualistic	stable	assisted	initiated	simplified
assertive	industrious	thorough	began	innovated	sold
astute	informal		budgeted	instructed	solved
bold	intellectual		built	introduced	staffed
broad-minded	intelligent		composed	invented	started
businesslike	inventive		conceived	launched	structured
calm	logical		conducted	led	streamlined
capable	methodical		completed	maintained	strengthened
careful	meticulous		consolidated	managed	stressed
competent	moderate		controlled	motivated	stretched
competitive	motivated		converted	negotiated	succeeded
confident	obliging		coordinated	operated	summarized
conscientious	organized		counseled	organized	supervised
conservative	outgoing		created	participated	supported
consistent	persevering		delegated	performed	taught
cooperative	pleasant		delivered	planned	terminated
creative	poised		demonstrated	prepared	traced
deliberate	polite		designed	presented	tracked

TABLE 9.2 (continued)

determined	practical	developed	processed	trained
discreet	precise	devised	produced	transferred
easy-going	progressive	directed	programmed	transformed
efficient	prudent	earned	promoted	translated
energetic	purposeful	edited	proposed	trimmed
experienced	quick	eliminated	provided	tutored
fair-minded	rational	ensured	purchased	uncovered
far-sighted	reflective	established	qualified	unified
firm	relaxed	evaluated	rated	verified
flexible	reliable	expanded	recommended	widened
focused	reserved	formulated	recruited	won
formal	resourceful	founded	redesigned	worked
friendly	responsible	generated	reduced	

EXERCISE 9.2 – ANNOTATIONS

Write an annotation for two or three entirely different entry types—for example, a help file, quick-reference card, proposal, professional presentation, documentation plan, usability test, etc. Each annotation should include the title, purpose, date developed, skills in a narrative format using the same words that appear in your resume, as well as the creation and delivery tools. Describe in detail the position you are seeking—skills, experience, technological proficiencies.

SELECTING ENTRIES FOR YOUR PORTFOLIO

The purpose of a portfolio is to demonstrate your proficiencies within the technical communication field. Therefore you should consider including any projects or skills that show the competencies that you want to market. Select only your best work for your portfolio. If you want to show a range of proficiencies, select your best sample from each of the included genres.

TABLE 9.3

REQUIRED ELEMENTS	POSSIBLE ENTRIES		
• Name and contact information • Resume • Prefatory statement • Annotated table of contents • Annotated entry cards: title, context, authors with percentage of work, skills and proficiencies, creation and delivery tools • Hyperlinks to documents	• Online help files • Wizards • Install guides • Instructional media • Storyboards • Grids/wireframes • Training material • Recommendation reports • Feasibility reports • Documentation plans • Release notes • Engineering specifications	• Product demos • Software simulations • User guides • Quick reference guides • Usability testing surveys and questionnaires • Professional articles and white papers • Style sheets and word lists • Style guides • Professional presentations and webinars	• Instructional podcasts • FAQs • Brochures and fliers • Layout or design projects • Marked-up editing pages • Web sites and pages • Revisions • Awards • Letters of recommendation • Academic transcripts

Paper Documentation

Paper documentation such as manuals, reference guides, and quick start cards work well in a portfolio when converted to an electronic medium like a Portable Document Format (PDF). A PDF file is a compressed document retaining all of the document's original fonts, graphics, colors, and layouts. Once converted, your audience will need a program to view the PDF file, such as Adobe Acrobat Reader.

Programs such as the Adobe Acrobat Reader and Flash Player display a document in its intended format—retaining all of the document's original fonts, graphics, colors, and layouts—while allowing you to prevent editing changes.

Instructional Podcasts

The annotations for a podcast should include the following information:

- Title
- Author(s)
- Keywords
- Abstract
- Running Time
- File Information (format, file size)
- Tool(s) Used to Create It

Webinars and Webcasts

A webinar is a presentation, lecture, workshop, or seminar that is transmitted over the web. For interactive online workshops web conferences are complemented by electronic meeting systems (EMS) which provide a range of online facilitation tools, such as brainstorming and categorization, and a range of voting methods or structured discussions, typically with optional anonymity.

When including a multimedia presentation in a portfolio, be sure to set the frame rate so that the reader will have enough time to read and/or hear the information before moving on to the next element. In addition you should always include instructions for exiting the presentation on your entry screen in case the reader does not wish to view the entire slide show.

Conference Presentations

Conferences often have proceedings with presentations published into a PDF and/or a hardcopy publication.

Online Help Files

Electronic help projects are easy to include in an electronic portfolio. For files that depend on viewing software, such as a browser and a Flash Player, you will need to indicate a player or viewer is necessary to view the documents and provide a link to download them.

Test each link thoroughly within your help file, and if you have broken links because of proprietary information or if you are including only an excerpt, be sure to note that in your entry screen. Consider writing a help file specifically for your portfolio to explain navigational elements, downloads, and viewing software that the reader may not be familiar with. This serves the dual purpose of providing immediate help for your reader as well as demonstrating your proficiency with online help-authoring programs.

White Papers

The entry card should include an abstract of the paper, keywords, and the file information: format, file size, number of pages, and whether the paper contains images. If the document resides online, provide a link to the URL.

Web Pages

For internet-based online portfolios, include active links to other web pages that you have created. Set the link to open the web page in a new browser window so that the reader does not have to leave your portfolio to review your work. Be sure to note on your entry screen how to return to your portfolio after viewing another web page.

For DVD or CD electronic portfolios, do not assume that your reader has an active internet connection. In addition to including links to the web page itself, include HTML files and a web browser, or screen captures of the web page. Always check your links to ensure that the web page displays correctly, and again be sure to note on your entry screen how to return to your portfolio after viewing the web page.

Video and Sound Files

Imbedded video and sound files can serve as a multimedia introduction to yourself and your portfolio as well as orienting the user to navigational elements. Be sure to rigorously test these files on computers with several different speeds. An impressive video clip ceases to be impressive when it jumps, skips, hangs, or locks up a computer. If you find that your video or sound files work on all but a few types of computers, make the file optional with a clickable link and explain potential problems in your entry screen. Include a stop or exit button in case the user does not want to watch or listen to the entire clip.

Multimedia Instructional Materials

Like online help files, software simulations, interactive demos, and tutorials of software or systems such as those created with Adobe Captivate, TechSmith Camtasia, and MadCap Mimic are easily integrated into an online portfolio. Consider using these tools to create a tutorial for your own portfolio. Again, this provides valuable help to the user in addition to demonstrating your proficiency.

Proposals

Proposals for grants, equipment, funding, and feasibility studies demonstrate your ability to research and write persuasive documents. Be sure to note if the proposal was approved, including specific amounts awarded. If the proposal was rejected due to circumstances unrelated to your proposal, note this fact in your entry screen.

Training Documentation

Training documentation such as handouts, packets, and instructions can be scanned and converted to PDF. On your entry screen list the number of training participants, the length of the training session, and the audience of the training.

Brochures and Flyers

Include only a few samples of brochures and flyers. Indicate which software program you used to produce the documents and whether a graphic designer contributed to the brochure or flyer. On your entry screen note the production run and distribution of the document.

Letters of Recommendation

Most employers want references with your resume, and the online portfolio allows you to include more than just contact information. Letters of recommendation can be one of the strongest elements in your portfolio when others are willing to speak on your behalf. Letters of recommendation should be on letterhead and include the writer's signature and contact information, including an email address.

Transcripts

If you are a recent graduate or if you have course work but no work experience that match a job ad, consider including your academic transcript in your portfolio. Your transcript shows the variety of courses you've completed, as well as your GPA. An unofficial transcript can be obtained and scanned in for your portfolio. If you choose to include an academic transcript, indicate it is unofficial but that you are happy to have the university send an official transcript if necessary.

LAYING OUT YOUR PORTFOLIO

A consistent approach to the layout of the entry card and annotations further reinforces the reader's sense of context within the document. Begin by gathering representative samples of your text and accompanying graphics, and experiment with different arrangements of the elements on the page. Your goal is to establish a consistent, logical page layout and design that will allow you to create a template to "plug in" content (text and graphics) without having to stop and rethink your basic design for each portfolio entry.

Grids

Grids are used in almost all professional magazines, books, newspapers, and website layouts to group and organize information consistently. You can combine or subdivide columns and rows to group or separate content by consistent increments.

Grids are visual standards that depict the layout and design of elements in paper or screen documents. Grids ensure consistency in the type, order, appearance, and placement of information on a page or interface.

Another benefit of using a grid structure is that you can move elements from page to page, but rather than seeming random, the movement will reference an underlying visual system. And in referencing the grid by moving elements in proportional and consistent increments, you establish a unifying and discernible pattern.

Alignment and proximity

By putting elements closer through the use of alignment and proximity, you create a contextual relationship. When you place elements along the same vertical or horizontal grid line, you create an invisible line connecting those elements. This visual line also creates a sense of movement and direction.

Sketching

Sketching is particularly helpful in developing grids. The simple act of quickly and loosely drawing out speculative combinations of rows and columns and potential layouts can save time and often leads to grid solutions rather than simply jumping ahead to designing or even coding a grid.

EXERCISE 9.3 – LAYOUT GRID & MATRIX

Create a PDF layout grid and layout and typography matrix for your portfolio's entry card annotations.

Your layout grid should include the following:

- Page or screen divided into columns and rows
- Grid modules

The layout and typography matrix should include the different visual elements:

- Graphic format – Tiff, jpeg, gif, or bitmap
- Graphic size – Resolution and dimension
- Typography – Typefaces, type styles, and point sizes of text
- Colors – Typefaces, leader lines, borders, and shading

Navigation

Navigation is typically composed of four core components:

- **Orientation** – Where am I am right now?
- **Route decisions** – Can I find the way to where I want to go?
- **Mental mapping** – Are my experiences consistent and understandable enough to know where I've been and to predict where I should go next?
- **Closure** – Can I recognize that I have arrived in the right place?

In portfolios, navigational paths should be clear, consistent, and predictable links that appear the same throughout the document.

Familiarity

Familiarity and memory play an important role in navigation, and later, usability. Visual design ensures that page elements are familiar and memorable.

Consistency

Consistency is the golden rule of interface design and wayfinding. A well-designed site navigation system is built on a consistent page grid, terminology, and navigation links, but it also incorporates the visual flexibility to create identifiable regions and edges within the larger space. In a corporate site, if you move from one region to another—say, from marketing to human resources—you ought to notice that you just passed an important regional boundary.

FIGURE 9.4

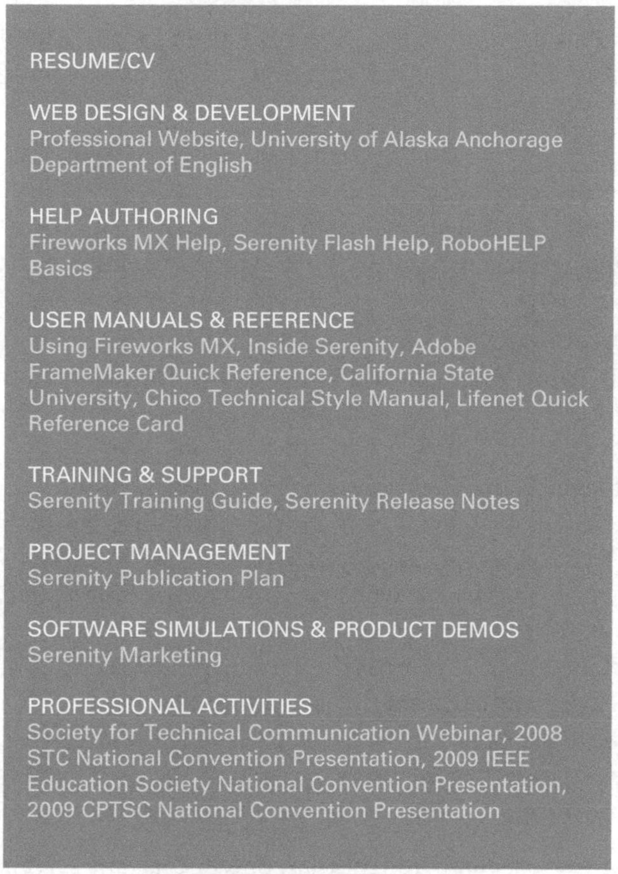

RESUME/CV

WEB DESIGN & DEVELOPMENT
Professional Website, University of Alaska Anchorage Department of English

HELP AUTHORING
Fireworks MX Help, Serenity Flash Help, RoboHELP Basics

USER MANUALS & REFERENCE
Using Fireworks MX, Inside Serenity, Adobe FrameMaker Quick Reference, California State University, Chico Technical Style Manual, Lifenet Quick Reference Card

TRAINING & SUPPORT
Serenity Training Guide, Serenity Release Notes

PROJECT MANAGEMENT
Serenity Publication Plan

SOFTWARE SIMULATIONS & PRODUCT DEMOS
Serenity Marketing

PROFESSIONAL ACTIVITIES
Society for Technical Communication Webinar, 2008 STC National Convention Presentation, 2009 IEEE Education Society National Convention Presentation, 2009 CPTSC National Convention Presentation

Navigation affordances

Characteristics that give clue of a link are called *perceived affordances*. For example, underlined text in an electronic document indicates a hyperlink. Regardless of the affordances you use, be consistent. The size, color, and style of links should be consistent throughout the site. It's appropriate to change affordances only if the meaning attached to the links change. For instance, a site might use green links and page backgrounds for all product pages and blue links and page backgrounds for all services pages.

Affordances for navigational images

- Symmetrical shapes circles, rectangles, ovals and rounded rectangles
- Drop shadows
- 3-D bevels that makes an element look like a raised or depressed button
- Grouping of some sort of symbol

Your design should indicate what is a clickable hyperlink and what is not. Language on links and buttons should be specific and understandable so users are confident that they are taking the right.

Vanishing Navigation

Vanishing navigation is a navigational infrastructure that isn't consistent throughout a site. This confuses readers, who must start over learning the navigation scheme.

Required navigational elements

At the very least, each page should include the following navigation aids to facilitate wayfinding:

- **Document identification –** Name and page identification
- **A link to the home page** – Although the portfolio identification or logo can serve as a link to the home page, there should be an explicit Home button as well. The user should always be able to go to the home page in a single click, regardless of where they are in the portfolio.
- **Contact information –** Your portfolio should include not only email contacts but also phone numbers and postal addresses.
- **Links to main pages under the home page** – These links are called *persistent navigation* because they are on every page of the document. They provide the user with a conceptual map of the document's structure and scope.

If your pages are consistently longer than one-and-a-half screens, duplicate navigational links at the bottom of your screens or pages to help readers navigate without forcing them to always scroll to the top of your pages.

EXERCISE 9.4 – NAVIGATION

Go online and find a portfolio that has effective navigation and another one that has poor navigation. Compare and contrast what the well-designed one did well that the other didn't do so well. How would you redesign the portfolio that has poor navigation?

LEGAL ISSUES

Because a company pays for your time and provides the resources to produce texts, the company is usually the sole copyright holder of texts you produce while in the company's employment. Be sure to get permission from the copyright holder for any information you use.

Statement of Originality and Confidentiality

The entries in this portfolio represent the work of (your name) and/or the work of groups I have worked with. In the cases where the work of others appears, I have included it with the permission of the original author.

In turn, you have the right to ask that viewers of the portfolio not duplicate your work.

> I respectfully request that the information contained in these documents not be duplicated or distributed.

Confidentiality and trade secrets

Traditionally companies concerned with sensitive information aggressively maintain their trade secrets through nondisclosure agreements, controlled or restricted access, and even more stringent steps to ensure intellectual property.

You should always look to gain written permission to use samples of your projects in your portfolio to avoid possible litigation for disclosing trade secrets. It is good practice to have written approval on file when you are unsure of using restricted information.

Proprietary information

Proprietary information is information that gives a company a competitive advantage over another or could be damaging if disclosed. Proprietary information typically includes the following, but since proprietary information is company-specific, ask your employer what information is considered proprietary:

- Source code
- Object code
- Schematics
- Presentational material
- Drafts of manuals
- Project code names and descriptions

A common practice is to black out sensitive material or proprietary information, but once again, look to gain written permission to avoid possibly disclosing proprietary information in your portfolio.

Copyright notices

An additional measure to ensure protection of intellectual property is have a copyright notice at the end of each of your entries and on a separate screen or page entitled "Copyright" or "Terms."

©Name, all rights reserved

You may include a permission disclaimer that provides contact information and how you wish to be acknowledged, should readers wish to use your material.

Trademarks

A trademark is a name, word, or phrase used to identify a particular brand of products or services made by a company and to distinguish them from those made by others. A trademark yet to be registered with the U.S. Patent and Trademark Office is identified with a ™ symbol. After the trademark has been registered, it is identified by the ® symbol. Some companies require that you contact them for permission to use their trademarks. Contact the companies if you are unsure of their guidelines.

When you use the name of a software program or its creator, you must ensure that it is trademarked at the first mention of the trademarked products and on pages and screens that are meant to be viewed sequentially.

This document was created with Adobe® RoboHELP® software.

In addition, you should have a screen that attributes trademarks to companies in a legend found on a separate screen at the end of the portfolio.

USABILITY TESTING

Especially with something as important as a career document, you should have as many as people as possible review your portfolio.

Test Types

These are typical types of tests:

- **"Get it" testing** – Show someone your portfolio to see if they understand how it is organized, how it works, and so on.
- **Key task testing** – Ask someone to do something, then watch how well they are able to do it. For example, you could ask them to find a specific piece of information.

With any type of usability testing, you should first try the test yourself and not become defensive if they criticize the document or an entry or are unable to find something.

Testing Organization

Test the overall organization of the document by asking subjects to draw a page- or node-link diagram of your portfolio after they have examined it. You may also ask two or three people to navigate through the hierarchy of your portfolio to find particular information.

Testing navigation and hyperlinks

Ask someone to pick out the hotspot (clickable) areas of your pages or screens and then predict the destinations of both text and icon links. In the case of icon links, ask participants to identify the object being represented and to explain what they think the icon means. Even if you plan to label your icons, you should test them without their labels to see how well the icon itself communicates.

Sample Usability Test Questions

The following are sample questions and exercises you can use during your usability tests:

1. What is your first impression of the portfolio?
2. Does the portfolio highlight skills and professional experience that support your career goals?
3. Where do you want to go after entering the portfolio?
4. Could you easily determine how to find more information about a subject?
5. Is the portfolio well organized? How may the organization be improved?
6. Did everything work as you expected?
7. What do you like/dislike about the portfolio?
8. Did you have trouble finding a particular element?
9. How many clicks did it take you to find what you were looking for?
10. Where are you? How can you tell?
11. How can you get back to the entry screen or page?

Test results and follow-up

Create a list of points so you don't forget what to address. Make sure you address these problems within a day or two after the test, when they are still fresh in your mind. In the next test pay close attention to the areas you changed. Do the test subjects still have problems? You will know you've fixed the problem if they don't notice it.

EXERCISE 9.5 – USABILITY TESTING

Recruit others to usability test your portfolio. They should test features such as:

- Content
- Design consistency
- Navigability
- Functionality
- Broken links
- Bookmarks
- Page numbering
- Navigation affordances
- All buttons, mouseovers, pop-ups, executable files, external files, and any effects

Test your portfolio on as many computers with as many profiles as you can:

- Windows
- Macintosh
- Unix or Linux

Set up your test for people with a wide variety of skill levels:

- Peers or willing coworkers
- Friends, family, neighbors
- A fourth grader

DISTRIBUTING YOUR ELECTRONIC PORTFOLIO

Include a cover letter with your portfolio—or the URL of your portfolio if it's online—on the enclosure line, and provide a copy of your resume as a file separate from your portfolio. For PDF portfolios, it's always a good idea to have an optimized version to distribute electronically in emails and on web sites. Additionally, include any requirements, viewers or players, or troubleshooting needed to run your portfolio.

PORTFOLIO BUILDER 9.1 – PROFESSIONAL PORTFOLIO

This final exercise entails designing, creating, and publishing a functional electronic portfolio in HTML, Flash, or PDF format. You should present three or four substantial samples of your work, each one prefaced with an annotation—a detailed statement that explains the circumstances under which you created it. You will also present a prefatory narrative that explains how the portfolio represents the range of your skills and experience.

The items should represent different genres; in other words, you will not present three user's manuals. A good portfolio is diverse and demonstrates a wide range of professional writing proficiencies.

Optimize graphics for online readability. Choose readable font types and sizes created specifically for online viewing, such as Georgia or Verdana. Always choose standard fonts (no Star Trek novelty typefaces) unless you know for sure that your fonts will be imbedded.

Credits

Image within Fig. 9.3: Copyright © by Google.

CPSIA information can be obtained
at www.ICGtesting.com
Printed in the USA
BVHW061043110920
588466BV00001B/21

9 781516 510290